A STEP-BY-STEP GUIDE TO THE PROPOSAL PROCESS

WINNING PROPOSALS

BY KAYE VIVIAN, ABC

Issued by the Management of an Accounting Practice Committee

AICPA
American Institute of Certified Public Accountants

2 3 4 5 6 7 8 9 0 PM 9 9 8 7 6 5 4 3

Library of Congress Cataloging-in-Publication Data

Vivian, Kaye.
  Winning proposals: a step-by-step guide to the proposal process/by Kaye Vivian; issued by the Management of an Accounting Practice Committee.
      p.   cm.
  Includes bibliographical references.
  ISBN 0-87051-128-9
  1. Accounting—Marketing. 2. Auditing—Marketing. 3. Proposal writing in business.
  I. American Institute of Certified Public Accountants. Management of an Accounting Practice Committee. II. Title.
HF5657.V55   1992
657'.068'8—dc20
                                                        92-42620
                                                          CIP

This book is dedicated to Abraham,
my inspiration and best friend,
and to Jim S. Ivy,
who showed me how success is measured by auditors.

Preface

The goal of this book is to help CPA firms win more proposals in an increasingly competitive environment. Proposals are the critical juncture of the selling process—they are the point at which a firm may win or lose a potential client.

Firms of different sizes approach proposals differently. This book focuses on major proposals for auditing and accounting services. The proposal process in most larger firms with multiple resources readily available will usually be more complex than the proposal process in smaller firms. However, the underlying concepts are the same, no matter how elaborate the techniques. To get the most from this book, the reader from a smaller firm should read the book with two purposes in mind:

1. To identify procedures that can be adapted to his or her firm
2. To gain insight into how other firms approach proposal opportunities

While your firm may not use all the guidance offered in every proposal situation, this book should be useful in evaluating and rethinking your current proposal activities.

Proposals are rarely the work of a single person. Most proposals are team efforts that involve administrative support, professional staff, and office management. Managing this effort effectively is a monumental task, but doing it well will help you to succeed more often and help your firm improve its bottom line.

Acknowledgments

These are some of the people to whom I am grateful, professionally and personally, for their generosity, wisdom, camaraderie, and good ideas: Amy Harwell, whose understanding of proposals and human nature brought us together and whose original ideas were the basis of many parts of this book; Bill Bancroft, Dave Crutcher, and George Michael.

Although I can't list them all, over the years I have worked on proposals with many unforgettable partners and managers, including Michael Budnick, Joe Murphy, Jim Ivy, Kevin Carton, Jay Brodish, Bob Panaro, Mark Sheeran, Jim Mitchell, Dan Garner, Tom Rich, Stan Gott, Mike Fischer, Steve Wagner, and Jim Quigley.

I have also worked on proposals with a talented bunch of marketing professionals: Trip Overholt, Richard Wellem, Laura Clime, Craig Minbiole, Nancie Mills, Joanne Broderick, Karol White, Irene Korsyn, Linda Russell, Linda Roberts, Kelly Villasuso, Shelly Ko, and Michele Bondy. Thanks to all of them for the special bonds proposals bring—the intensity of sharing something significant and the immense relief when it is over.

Finally, a special thank you to Laura Inge at the AICPA for her delicacy, wisdom, and strong encouragement, and to Masha Zipper and the outstanding librarians at the national office of Price Waterhouse.

The following are the members of the Management of an Accounting Practice Committee Task Force and others who provided direction for and reviews of this book:

James R. Beers, CPA
Task Force Chairman
Beers & Cutler
Washington, DC

Glen S. Adamec
Marketing Coordinator
Ross, Langan & McKendree CPAs
McLean, Virginia

Robert J. Batson, CPA
Batson Carnahan Doyle & Co., P.A.
Fort Myers, Florida

T. Elonide Caldwell Semmes, CPA
Marketing Director
Beers & Cutler
Washington, DC

Lucy R. Carter, CPA
Carter, Young, Wolf, Davis
  & Dahlhauser
Nashville, Tennessee

John M. Hughes, Jr., CPA
Levine, Hughes & Mithuen, Inc.
Englewood, Colorado

Charles E. Keller, III, CPA
Keller, Zanger, Bissell & Co.
Frederick, Maryland

Thomas P. Langan, CPA
Ross, Langan & McKendree CPAs
McLean, Virginia

Colette Nassutti
Marketing Consultant
San Jose, California

Mahlon Rubin, CPA
Rubin, Brown, Gornstein & Co.
St. Louis, Missouri

Rebecca K. Seidman
Marketing Director
Walpert Smulliam & Blumthal, P.A.
Baltimore, Maryland

Abram J. Serotta, CPA
Serotta, Maddocks & Devanny, P.C.
Augusta, Georgia

Judith R. Trepeck, CPA
Rehmann Robson & Co.
Farmington Hills, Michigan

Alfred W. Walpert, CPA
Walpert Smulliam & Blumthal, P.A.
Baltimore, Maryland

Anne M. Wright
Marketing Director
Keller, Zanger, Bissell & Co.
Frederick, Maryland

AICPA Staff:

Nancy R. Myers, Director
Practice Management Division

Laura E. Inge, Project Manager
Practice Management Division

Table of Contents

Chapter 1:
Introduction

Ask any ten people what a proposal is and nine of the ten will say "a document." A proposal is much more than a document—it is a process of persuasive communication. The proposal process begins when you are given a proposal opportunity or receive a request for proposal (RFP). It does not end until the prospective client makes a decision.

Advance Preparations

Each proposal varies according to the needs of the prospective client. Nevertheless, there are advance preparations a firm can make to expedite the proposal process.

NETWORKING

One crucial factor in the proposal process that must be undertaken even before an actual proposal opportunity is in sight is the development of business relationships. Contact development is a vital part of any firm's marketing efforts and will frequently determine the winner in a proposal opportunity. At the very least, contacts will get your firm in the door in situations where you might not have been an obvious choice.

All firms need a marketing program designed to help them identify and build relationships with executives of selected companies they would like to have as clients. Developing contacts within a prospective organization enables your firm to gain a friendly edge over other competing firms by means of an established relationship with one or more of the executive decision makers. Don't wait until your firm has been approached for a proposal to begin the networking process. At that point, it may be too late.

IDENTIFY
YOUR OFFICE'S
PROPOSAL "GURU"

It is important for firm members to know who is the proposal expert in their office. In most offices, there is at least one partner who has participated in several significant proposal efforts. Make this expert available to proposal teams to provide shortcuts, insight, tips, pointers, and general guidance for those less experienced. It is also a good idea to have this person present at rehearsals for important client meetings and oral presentations to critique both content and delivery.

ESTABLISH A
PROPOSAL
RESOURCE
CENTER

It's not necessary to re-invent the wheel every time you write a proposal. A member of your marketing or administrative staff, with the guidance of your firm's proposal expert, could be responsible for establishing and maintaining a collection of reference material.

Reference materials that may be useful when developing a proposal include the following.

Information on Proposals

- Copies of your firm's past proposals (filed alphabetically by company name and cross-indexed by industry) for the past two to three years. Include the name of the prospective client and year of the proposal on the file label.

- Copies of other firms' proposals.

- Sample proposal text or a text data base that provides a benefits-oriented description of your firm's capabilities in every service and industry specialization (see chapter 4 for a discussion of benefits versus features) and reasons to change (or not to change) the firm.

- All relevant materials, such as forms and checklists used in the proposal process, and, if it exists, the firm's graphic standards guidelines.

- Sample requests for proposals from various organizations.

Information on Your Firm's Personnel

- Copies of full biographies of all partners and key managers (such as industry specialists), perhaps contained in a three-ring binder. Some firms maintain this data base in their word-processing department. Update the information at least annually.

- Photographs of all partners and managers. Arrange for a standard pose and background so that the photos will have a professional appearance when used together. Keep at least three 5 x 7 copies of each on hand and use them for publicity announcements as well. Take new pictures at least every two years.

- Up-to-date list of all personnel and their billing rates. At larger firms, these can be sorted in different ways, such as by office, level, and discipline.

Information on Your Firm's Operations

- Standard information—such as a description of the firm, its offices, philosophy of client service, peer review, and litigation record—should be put into a format that can be used in any proposal. Having this boilerplate text available streamlines the writing exercise for everyone.

- A list of all your firm's various services and a supply of general or services brochures and newsletters.

- Examples of distinctive features that can differentiate your firm from others. This list will serve as a quick reminder when you are immersed in the proposal process. Examples of such features include—
  — A unique service specialty.

— The expertise of a recognized industry expert or authority on your staff.

— International affiliations.

— Generalist partners who do both audit work and tax work, so that the client has to deal with only one person.

— Excellent results from client satisfaction surveys.

— Cost-effective techniques or training that can help control fees.

— Frequency or types of communications with client management and boards.

IDENTIFY MARKETING REFERENCE MATERIAL

To ensure that you do not overlook other valuable information when proposing, conduct a survey of the materials maintained by your firm's marketing department and library. Items that can provide helpful, or even significant, insights include the following.

Information on Your Firm's Market Share

Organizations such as Dun's Marketing (a subsidiary of Dun & Bradstreet) offer microcomputer-based listings containing local data for an annual fee to assist firms preparing their own analysis. If the firm is large, it may have or can develop information on auditor market share from published sources such as the following:

- *Business Week*'s America's 70 most competitive companies

- *Business Week*'s 100 best small companies

- *Business Week*'s 1000 most valuable companies

- *Datamation*'s 100

- Dow-Jones' 30 industrials

- *Forbes*' 200 best small companies

- *Forbes*' 400 largest private companies

- *Fortune*'s 500 leading industrial companies

- *Fortune*'s 500 leading service companies

- *Fortune*'s 50 leading exporters

- *Inc.*'s 100 fastest growing small public companies

- Standard & Poor's 500

- Local business journals' lists of the top twenty-five companies in your city or area

- *Audit Trak* lists auditor changes in public companies and the reasons for the changes; cumulates all changes on a quarterly and annual basis

- Other geographic and industry-specific lists available for purchase, such as *Crain's New York Business* or the MAPI analysis of audit fees paid by manufacturing companies

- In industries where your firm has special expertise, the listings of leading trade publications can be used to develop market share information

Information on Your Firm's Competitors

An important tactic in the proposal process is to know your competition. There are numerous sources for obtaining information on your competitors:

- Accounting profession newsletters, newspapers, and journals
  - *Public Accounting Report*
  - *Emerson's Professional Services Review*
  - *Bowman's Accounting Report*
  - *International Accounting Bulletin*
  - *World Accounting Report*
  - *CPA Marketing Report*
  - *CPA Computer Report*
  - *CPA Personnel Report*
  - AAM (Association for Accounting Marketing) *MarketTrends*
  - *The Marcus Report*
  - *Accounting Office and Administrative Report*
- News wires, business journals, newspapers
- On-line (Commercial Data Base) resources—Most of these data bases are searchable using accounting firm names.
- Major business journals—Remember to check *The Wall Street Journal, The New York Times, Forbes, Fortune, Business Week, Inc., Venture*, and other national and regional publications. Most of these are available from on-line data bases as well.
- Accounting firms' publications—Competitors' brochures, newsletters, and booklets should not be overlooked. Many firms are willing to send copies of their brochures if you just call and ask.

Information on Your Firm's Client Base

- Up-to-date copy of your firm's full client list, by company name, partner name, Standard Industrial Classification (SIC) code, type of work, and office and/or region.
- A list of major clients gained and lost in the past three to five years, with reasons for the gain or loss.

Information on Your Firm's Prospective Clients

- Files containing all press clippings, notes to file, and other pertinent material for each of your firm's targeted prospective clients.
- A data base of firm contacts. Qualify the degree to which each staff person knows that contact (for example, close personal friend, casual acquaintance, business colleague).

Although identifying a proposal "guru," establishing a proposal resource center, and identifying useful marketing references are potentially time-consuming, the investment will be rewarded with each proposal opportunity. Advance preparation can provide a foundation of expertise and information that will assist your firm at each stage in the proposal process.

The Proposal Process

The proposal process may take anywhere from a few days to several months. During that time, you will be working on the written proposal and will usually visit a business' operations, meet with members of management, establish a fee estimate, and make one or more oral presentations.

The process for each proposal usually includes these stages:

Step 1: Address the preliminary strategic issues

   a. Evaluate the opportunity
   - Verify that the prospective client meets your firm's new client acceptance criteria
   - Categorize the proposal opportunity as major or standard

   b. Select the proposal team and assign duties

   c. Research the prospective client
   - Identify important management issues
   - Determine fee history, significance of fees, and the competition
   - Assess potential litigation risk

   d. Make the go/no-go decision

Step 2: Organize management meetings and site visits

   a. Attend management meetings
   - Identify the decision-making unit's roles
   - Identify the decision makers' needs

   b. Conduct site visits
   - Send an introductory letter
   - Prepare questions
   - Investigate the prospective client through site interviews
   - Debrief team members

Step 3: Develop a win strategy

   a. Conduct a strategic analysis; if reproposal, evaluate service issues
   - Outline decision makers' needs using the 12 C's selection criteria
   - Identify all contacts in prospective client's organization

   b. Define the win strategy
   - Review the decision makers' needs
   - Brainstorm

Step 4: Produce the proposal document

   a. Determine format and content of the proposal document

   b. Draft the proposal document
   - Coordinate the writing and editing of drafts

- Determine graphics and artwork for cover and tabs
- Secure outside artist or consultants, if needed
- Deliver advanced draft to review team
- Ensure that all items in the RFP are addressed
- Review document strategy against overall proposal strategy and sign off

c. Print the proposal document
- Establish a production schedule for graphics, artwork and printing
- Deliver final proposal text to printing
- Bind the proposal document
- Deliver the proposal document to prospective client
- Follow up with prospective client and receive feedback, taking action if needed

SELECTION DECISION POINT: *[Prospective client selects firms for continued consideration or makes final selection.]*

Step 5:   Deliver the oral presentation

a. Organize the oral presentation
- Review and revise strategy
- Identify the audience
- Determine content
- Select speakers and establish rehearsal schedule
- Determine presentation format
- Determine needed visual aids and establish production timetable

b. Hold full-team dress rehearsal/coaching sessions

c. Make presentation

d. Follow up with prospective client after the presentation

SELECTION DECISION POINT: *[Prospective client selects firm.]*

Step 6:   Do a postmortem evaluation

a. Follow up with prospective client after the presentation

b. Notify firm personnel of gain/loss

c. Conduct a postmortem interview
- Debrief prospective client
- Leave the door open for future work

d. Draft and distribute a postmortem summary

While this process appears linear, in reality stages may overlap, occur concurrently, or be omitted altogether. Every proposal situation is different from all others.

Chapter 2:
The First Stages of the
Proposal Process

While each proposal process is different, there are some basic tasks that should be undertaken almost immediately at every proposal opportunity. Time and energy spent at this stage will pay off in a more effective proposal later.

Opportunity Knocks

A request for proposal (RFP) may come through the mail unsolicited or it may come as a result of your firm's marketing efforts. It may be in the form of a short letter or a lengthy request asking for specific information about your firm. A lengthy request is usually used by larger, more experienced companies. It often spells out in detail what management needs to know about your firm in order to make its selection. (Sample RFPs are provided in appendix A.)

An RFP may also come in the form of a telephone call to someone in your firm. Some prospective clients, especially small to midsize companies, may not be experienced in asking for competitive proposals and will leave it up to the proposing firm to determine the nature and extent of information to include in the proposal.

Regardless of whether or not the prospective client asks for specific information, it is always your firm's responsibility to discover the prospective client's needs and to provide information that you think will persuade the client to select your firm.

Evaluate the Opportunity

Your firm is not obligated to submit a proposal for every opportunity that comes along. As soon as the proposal opportunity appears, a careful evaluation should be made. Proposing can be an expensive investment. Therefore, when a proposal opportunity appears, you should make a preliminary decision as to whether the prospective client meets your criteria and fits into your strategic plan for new accounts. Also, if your firm is not willing to commit the resources needed to prepare a thorough, professional proposal, it may produce an inferior and potentially injurious one. Therefore, give careful, complete consideration to whether your firm should accept a proposal opportunity. If there are no compelling reasons to propose, bow out early and save your firm time and money.

To put proposal opportunities into perspective, categorize each one as either a major or standard opportunity. For example, a firm might define a major proposal as any opportunity for which recurring fees are $50,000 or more. A chance to get into a new industry or service line might be considered a major opportunity, even if the fee is relatively small. If a proposal opportunity is identified as major, your firm must then make a commitment to use the best resources available, internally or externally, to create a winning proposal. For standard opportunities, a more generic proposal response may suffice.

If you decide to propose, assemble the proposal team and direct it to move ahead. Remember, this decision is based on the best information you have on hand. It is a business decision that should be readdressed once the proposal team has properly researched the prospective client, the opportunity, and the competition. If the decision is not to propose, the firm should let the prospective client know immediately that it will not be submitting a proposal.

Select the Proposal Team and Assign Duties

The selection of the team is often based on the availability of professionals in the office. However, availability will not impress a prospective client. One of the most important criteria for the prospective client when selecting a new accounting firm is the specific industry experience of the proposal team members. Therefore, choose your team strategically and consider a potential proposal team member's knowledge of the industry and contacts within the prospective client's organization.

For an audit proposal, the proposed client-service team typically includes the lead audit partner, an audit manager, tax partner, or manager, and—if needed—the office managing partner. In large firms, the team frequently also includes a senior audit partner and a management consultant partner or industry specialist. This client service team, together with your marketing staff (if you have any) and your office's proposal "guru," will make up the proposal team.

The *team leader* is usually the proposed lead engagement partner, although it may be another individual—for example, an industry specialist who has a pre-existing relationship with the prospective client. The team leader is responsible for guiding the proposal team through the entire proposal process, as outlined in chapter 1. Therefore, he or she must be available to participate fully in the proposal process and provide strong team leadership.

Depending on the size of the firm, the proposal team leader often assigns the task of managing the proposal process to the proposed audit manager, but a member of the administrative or marketing staff may also serve in this role.

The *proposal coordinator* is responsible for organizing prospective client research (in step 1 of the proposal process outlined in chapter 1) and maintaining production schedules when developing the proposal document and the oral presentation (steps 4 and 5 in the proposal process outline). This assistance helps to keep the client-service team focused on strategic issues and meetings with the prospective client.

Research the Prospective Client

In order to make a meaningful proposal and to decide whether or not the prospective client is right for your firm, before committing the firm to the time and expense of site visits, the proposal team must gather as much information as possible about the prospective client's industry, organization, and staff participating in the selection process. The proposal team should specifically consider the following questions: Can the firm respond to the prospective client's management issues? Can the firm compete on fees? Is the prospective client a potential litigation risk?

RESEARCH ON MANAGEMENT ISSUES

When identifying industry issues and trends facing the management of the prospective client's company, certain issues will be obvious, while others may take more digging. Exhibit 2.1 provides some suggestions on what to look for and where.

Exhibit 2.1

Identifying the Important Issues

To find information on:	Check:
Industry trends	• Trade publications • Industry research studies • Trade association libraries • Interview with a competitor of the prospect
Corporate trends	• Annual reports. Compare prior three years and note the key words and leadership changes. Read between the lines for what is not being said.
Management concerns	• Speeches of chairman of the board/president • Analysts' reports • Articles by company officers • Personal interviews • Internal newsletters

(Continued on next page.)

Exhibit 2.1   *Identifying the Important Issues (Continued)*

To find information on:	Check:
Company-specific matters	• Expert opinions • Other industry leaders • Your firm's industry specialist • Prospect's alumni working for your company • Bankers • Lawyers • Public affairs staff • Consultants (such as PR firms and advertising firms) who have performed work for the company or its competitors.
If you notice—	*Find out—*
A shift in emphasis in the company or industry	• If the change was caused by internal policies and operations or by external pressures. • What kind of business activity the change has generated. • What problems the change has caused.
Management changes	• What triggered them. • The backgrounds of new members of the management team. • What effect the new team will have on the company's operations.

Most of the research material you need on larger corporations, organizations, and individuals can be found in reference books or commercially available on-line data bases. Effective research on family-owned or privately held businesses that have no regulated filing requirement can be difficult. For smaller businesses, too, you will find little published data. For these companies, it may be difficult to get information other than that available from the company's product brochure, unless you know an insider in the company who is willing to share with you the company's mission or goals and an organization chart. Discreet inquiries among local business leaders might also result in useful information. The data typically required for the early stages of proposal development may be gathered from a number of sources. Some of the more accessible sources are in appendix B.

To organize the information your proposal team uncovers, the Prospective Client Needs/Issues Assessment Form in exhibit 2.2 provides a model worksheet. Use it to identify where you need more information and to develop specific questions to ask members of management in your meetings and site visits. Revise this assessment each time you get new information and refer to it when proposing additional services to help the prospective client achieve its long-term goals.

Exhibit 2.2   *Prospective Client Needs/Issues Assessment Form (For Internal Use)*

Company Name: _____

Primary Industry: _____

Industry Issues: _____

_____

_____

Secondary Industry: _____

Industry Issues: _____

_____

_____

Management Concerns: _____

_____

_____

Corporate Issues: _____

_____

_____

Key Issues to Be Addressed	*Why Important?*	*Include in Proposal?*
1.		
2.		
3.		
4.		
5.		
6.		
7.		
8.		
9.		
10.		

RESEARCH ON FEES

When setting fees, the proposal team considers many in-house factors, such as the estimated hours and cost of personnel to perform the job. Three additional factors to consider during the research stage that can influence fees are—

1. Fee history of the prospective client.
2. Significance of fees to the prospective client.
3. Competition for the prospective client.

Fee History

It is always helpful to know what the prospective client is currently paying in fees. To obtain this information, the proposal team can candidly ask the prospective client what fees have been paid in the past. Normally, prospective clients are willing to share this information or at least give a range.

If a publicly traded company declines to share fee information, it is sometimes possible to determine its fee history by reviewing recent years' proxy statements. Companies are not required to disclose fees paid, but they occasionally do. For privately held or family businesses, it is more difficult to determine fee history, because the scope of the work can vary dramatically and these businesses have no statutory filing requirements. Here is where industry experts can be helpful. Their experience usually spans many different situations, and they can assess the scope of the work and estimate probable fees.

Significance of Fees

In the earliest meetings with the prospective client, the proposal team determines the significance of fees to the prospective client. The proposal team needs to know whether the prospective client is unhappy with current fee levels or is concerned about value received for fees paid. The proposal team should also listen closely in early fee discussions for clues that may provide guidance on the content and format of the fee presentation in the proposal document.

Competition

When establishing the fee, the proposal team analyzes the competition by considering the following questions: Does any one firm have a particular desire to obtain this prospective client? Is any competing firm trying to establish its credentials in this prospect's industry? If the answer is "yes" to either question, there is a good possibility that the competing firm will present a very low fee, viewing it as an investment. Although there is much discussion in the profession today about "buying audits" and "low balling," there are no rules to prevent such competitive activities.

RESEARCH ON PROSPECTIVE CLIENT'S RISK

In today's litigious society, a firm cannot be overly cautious when screening a prospective client. Most firms have established guidelines for client acceptance. Recommended guidelines for client screening include the following.[1] (Be sure to

---

[1] Adapted from Mark F. Murray, *Managing the Malpractice Maze* (New York: AICPA, 1992), p. 69.

complete these steps in advance of submitting a proposal, to avoid the embarrassment of withdrawing later.)

1. Determine why the prospective client is changing accountants.

2. Ask the prospective client's management for references and conduct an informal background check to determine their reputation for honesty, credit history and rating, financial stability, cooperativeness and litigation history, potential conflicts of interest, quality of management, competency of personnel, personality, and potential as sources of new clients. (Most large firms have detailed forms that can be used for this purpose.)

3. Determine whether the prospective client's industry or the services requested are high risk.

4. After receiving any necessary authorization, contact the prospective client's former accountant, as well as attorney, bankers, credit bureaus, present and former business associates, and employees. Inquiries to the Better Business Bureau, Chamber of Commerce, or an applicable trade association can be especially productive.

Remember, however, that even if the prospective client passes the screening with flying colors, client assessment does not stop there. It continues through the proposal process, and in fact, a major goal during site visits is to assess potential risk areas. Specific guidelines for client screening during the upcoming site visits include—

- Determining the condition of the prospective client's management, finances, and internal controls.

- Meeting the prospective client's accounting and tax personnel to determine specific financial needs and the condition of accounting records.

Make the Go/No-Go Decision

The proposal team must consider the cost of proposing (with all the time and energy it requires) versus the probability of winning and the value of the prospective client to the firm. The go/no-go worksheet in exhibit 2.3 can help the proposal team decide whether it is cost-effective for your firm to submit a proposal. In today's competitive environment and economy, electing to withdraw and save limited resources is often a wise business decision.

Exhibit 2.3   *The Go/No-Go Decision*

Company Name: _____

Work required: _____

Potential for additional work: _____

Year end: _____ Fees to be included in proposal?   Yes   No

Est. first year's fees: $_____ Est. discount expected (%): _____

Est. hrs. to complete proposal: _____

Total est. cost to propose: $_____

Competition (other firms):

Their Strengths/Weaknesses	*Our Response*
_____	_____
_____	_____
_____	_____

Our major weakness: _____

Our major strength: _____

Probable key decision makers: _____

Our relationship with each of them:

Other Firms	*Relationship*
_____	_____
_____	_____
_____	_____

Arguments against proposing: _____
_____

Do they meet our new-client acceptance criteria?   Yes   No
Why/Why Not? _____

Any special considerations: _____
_____
_____

Final decision: Propose   Decline to Propose

Recommended by: _____ Decision approved by: _____

Chapter 3:
Management Meetings
and Site Visits

Management meetings and site visits are your proposal team's best opportunity to discover the prospective client's criteria for selecting a CPA firm. The key to obtaining this information is *to ask what you need to know*. Many professionals have the false idea that questioning the prospective client about the selection process or competitive issues is unprofessional. But remember, to win the proposal you need to know more than competing firms know about this company. There is every reason for your proposal team to ask the questions necessary to understand and address the prospective client's concerns.

Attend Management Meetings

Management meetings are interviews with the prospective client's top management personnel in their offices. Such meetings can be held at the request of the prospective client or at the request of your firm. At these meetings, the discussion focuses on big-picture issues. You may have management meetings early on in the proposal process. In some instances, you may have several such meetings even before the RFP arrives.

The number of management meetings held during the proposal process varies widely with each proposal. Some prospective clients limit the number of management meetings in an effort to be fair to all proposing firms. In many cases, the prospective client's willingness or unwillingness to meet with you indicates its interest in your firm, particularly if you are being avoided while the prospective client continues to meet with a competing firm. The more meetings you have the better, since management meetings offer the best chance for the prospective client to develop a one-on-one relationship with your proposal team. For this reason, the proposal team should not be shy about requesting meetings with a prospective client. Time spent face-to-face is much more productive than time spent editing a document.

In this regard, smaller firms may have an advantage, since their members are more likely to have worked together on many jobs and feel a natural camaraderie. This team spirit and relaxed collegiality is reassuring to prospective clients. It is logical that the more comfortable your proposal team members are working with each other, the more confident they will appear and the more at ease your prospective client will feel working with each of you.

IDENTIFY THE ROLES OF VARIOUS DECISION MAKERS

In the proposal process, the decision maker is often assumed to be one individual who will say "yes" or "no." Although this may be true in smaller companies or closely held family businesses, more often than not the so-called decision maker is actually several people who make up a decision-making unit, or DMU.

It is important to use management meetings to identify all members of the DMU, to assess each one's personal and business reasons for selecting or rejecting your firm, and to determine the role each DMU member will play in the selection process.

Exhibit 3.1 summarizes the DMU—its members and their roles. But remember, every proposal is different and it is not necessary for every role to be played out in each proposal situation.

Exhibit 3.1   *The Decision-Making Unit*

DMU Member	*Role*	*Relationship-Building Methods*
Primary Decision Maker The one to whom all others defer, usually the CEO; the one who can say "Yes!"	Generally controls the budget or the function; the head of a family-owned business	Develop relationship prior to a proposal situation. Demonstrate confidence.
Influencer Often a long-time friend or associate of the primary decision maker	May have the ear of the real boss; can tip the scales in favor of one firm among equals	Provide examples of how you have helped others to succeed. The influencer is often under-utilized in the proposal process.
Advocate May be an alumnus or personal contact	Will speak out on your behalf when the DMU meets behind closed doors	Arm the advocate with all the benefits and facts needed to make your firm's case effectively in your absence.
Veto Voter Often has a personal reason to prefer another firm	May influence the other DMU members not to accept your proposals	Neutralize any potential objections, especially by addressing the veto voter's concerns in front of the assembled DMU during the oral presentation.

Exhibit 3.1   ***The Decision-Making Unit (Continued)***

DMU Member	Role	Relationship-Building Methods
Evaluator Usually in mid-management; often the contact you know the best	Reviews and weighs the various proposals against the selection criteria and makes a recommendation; may or may not be a part of the final selection process	Encourage him or her to reveal the selection criteria so that you can position yourself in the best possible way.
Gatekeeper Often a secretary or special assistant	Monitors access to the key decision maker; not usually part of the selection process	Develop a friendship and acknowledge his or her importance; treat with respect.

It is important to realize that the DMU can change members and that the members can change roles during the proposal process. In fact, it is common for the members of the DMU to change between the written proposal stage and the oral presentation stage. Except in the case of small or family-owned businesses, the proposal document evaluators are rarely the final decision makers. For example, at the written proposal stage, the head of internal audit and the director of tax frequently function as the key decision makers, deciding which firms may continue to compete in the oral presentation. During the oral presentation, when the CEO and chairperson of the audit committee join the DMU as primary decision makers, the other DMU members' roles will become less influential.

Successful proposal teams anticipate this fact and re-evaluate the DMU and each member's role at each step of the proposal process to reflect the participation of more senior decision makers.

IDENTIFY DECISION MAKERS' NEEDS

Depending on the size of the prospective client and the complexity of the circumstances, the types of questions a DMU member might ask in judging your firm include the following:

- Do we need the prestige of a major accounting firm to help us raise money?
- Will we get the hand-holding we need when our projects are smaller than those of other, larger clients that may compete for our accountant's time?
- Is this accounting firm sufficiently general-purpose to serve multiple needs, or does it rely on teams of high-priced specialists who will come and go?
- Is the firm big enough to handle our developing needs?
- Will the people doing the proposing be the ones who actually do the work?

- Personal relationships with our accountants are paramount. Do we like this team and do they have a working style like ours?
- Can the firm take us public?
- Does the firm work for any of our direct competitors?
- Does the firm have local or regional contacts or clients who can be of help to us?
- Who will the firm view as its client—our management? the board? our shareholders?
- Is the firm's fee within our budget range?
- Do they understand my business? Do they have experience or will we be expected to teach them?
- Will they disrupt my staff and daily business while they are here?

Your goal is to gain a "yes" vote from as many DMU members as possible when they meet without you to discuss your proposal and make their ultimate decision. People rarely make decisions rationally. Social scientists have shown that people make decisions emotionally and later find rational justifications to support them. A winning proposal takes into account not only the corporate or business interests, but also the personal interests of the DMU members, whether articulated or not. Successful proposals provide the answer for each DMU member to the question "What's in it for me?" This is accomplished by evaluating your firm's relationship with each member of the DMU—by identifying not only the business goals of key members of the DMU, but their personal goals as well.

Business goals of DMU members might include—

- Bringing a project in under budget.
- Initiating three new projects in this fiscal year.
- Meeting a quota or deadline.
- Installing a new financial reporting system.
- Downsizing a department.

Personal goals of DMU members might include—

- Getting a promotion, raise, or bonus.
- Being recognized as experts in their fields.
- Improving their own visibility at the highest levels.
- Doing work without error and on schedule.

Whenever your proposal fails to anticipate a DMU member's concern about what's in it for him or her, your chance of success diminishes. Therefore, you must attempt to identify these factors, even if you do not have all the facts. For example, you may not know for certain that a prospective client is interested to know how your firm's other clients could help his or her company, but you may conclude that this is the case based on your experience with similar businesses.

Your goals at management meetings include identifying—

1. The decision-making process.
2. The members of the decision-making unit.
3. The prospective client's expectations for its accounting firm.
4. The prospective client's organizational goals, needs, and objectives.
5. The prospective client's management goals, needs, and objectives.

Following each management meeting, proposal team members who were present need to discuss thoroughly the information and impressions obtained during the meeting. Different team members may interpret the prospective client's comments differently, so it is important to come to as accurate an understanding of the prospective client's needs and circumstances as possible.

Conduct Site Visits

A site visit is any meeting at the prospective client's headquarters or production facilities. Particularly for larger prospective clients, they are opportunities for the members of the proposal team to meet midlevel and operations management members, to observe their production processes, and to judge whether the organization is as it was represented to you by top management. Members of top management—such as the prospective client's CFO or vice-president of operations—may also attend. The proposal team may need to request a site visit but, as a rule, the prospective client assumes that any proposing firm will want to tour certain of their facilities. Your goals at a site visit include identifying—

- Audit risk.
- Potential problems.
- Critical business and industry issues for the organization and its leaders.
- Factors that will influence the selection of a firm.

In your efforts to uncover what makes this company tick, it is often revealing to obtain a range of answers by asking the same questions posed at the management meeting.

To be effective, a site visit should also include gathering insights into—

- The prospective client's expectations for its accounting firm.
- The prospective client's selection criteria.
- The decision-making process at the prospective client organization.

- The decision makers at the prospective client organization and their roles in decision making.

Site visits have two other significant purposes. They are your proposal team's best opportunity to—

1. Impress the prospective client (who often does not know you) with your working style.
2. Gain advocates through rapport.

Since the costs of site visits are paid by your firm, they are often limited in number. Even when proposing to a large company, site visits rarely exceed five—except when there are significant international operations. Therefore, you need to make the most of every site visit. The best way to take advantage of these valuable opportunities is through careful planning and preparation.

Gathering this amount of information can be time consuming (in terms of both preparation and time spent on the visit itself), but it will be worth the investment when it comes time to write your proposal. More important, advance preparation says something about you and your firm. It says that you are concerned about the overall functioning of the organization, not just about the numbers. Today, top management wants advisors who see the big picture. If you can impress the prospective client with your businesslike approach and attention to details, you will greatly increase your chances of winning the work.

SEND AN INTRODUCTORY LETTER

To make a good first impression, send an introductory personal letter to each operations person you are scheduled to meet. This letter might suggest a tentative agenda and tell the recipient what you want to see, other people you may want to meet, information you hope to obtain, and any topics you would like to discuss. To identify topics for a site visit, the proposal team reviews all information gathered from background research and management meetings to identify any gaps. As a courtesy, all topics of discussion should be cleared in advance with the prospective client's top management. Top management should also receive copies of any correspondence from the proposal team to personnel at the prospective client company.

The introductory letter has the following three purposes:

1. It is an act of courtesy that demonstrates a considerate working style.
2. It introduces proposal team members who will attend the site visit.
3. It gives the prospective client's personnel an opportunity to prepare for the interview.

Exhibit 3.2 is a sample letter that could be sent prior to a site visit.

Exhibit 3.2   *Introductory Letter*

Lead Partner
ABC Auditors
Address
Date

Operations Manager
XYZ Corporation
Address

Dear _____:

As you know, our firm is proposing to become the auditors of XYZ Corporation. John Smith told me that you have agreed to meet with us on March 15th at 2:30 p.m. so that we can see your facilities and ask you some questions.

John has explained that your time now is limited because of the quarterly report. To be sure that we make the best possible use of our time together, I have attached a list of topics we would like to cover. You may also have some questions you would like to ask us.

Kathryn Turner, an audit manager with nearly five years of experience working with high-tech manufacturing businesses, will accompany me to this meeting. I have enclosed our brief background biographies so you may learn something about us. We are both pleased to have the chance to meet you and talk about your operation. See you on the 15th.

Sincerely yours,

Lead Partner

Encl.

The following is a list of information the proposal team might request in the introductory letter:

- Copies of any of the following:
  - SEC filings
  - Corporate mission statement
  - Published speeches of the chairman or president
  - Corporate strategic plan
  - Materials related to any company-wide personnel programs and benefits
  - Copies of corporate tax returns and related information for the past two years (if a privately held company)
- Names of internal audit and tax staff

- Any information that will help us obtain a basic understanding of your operations and activities
- Internal reporting systems
- Anticipated financial changes in the coming year
- Inventory and production methods
- Anticipated manufacturing or systems changes
- Staffing changes recently made or anticipated in the coming year
- Concerns relating to the transition to new accountant services
- Factors expected to have an impact on the business or industry in the next five years
- Corporate growth strategy
- Preferred working relationship with auditors
- Criteria for selecting new auditors
- Decision-making process

PREPARE A LIST OF QUESTIONS

To extract valuable information from the prospective client during the site visit, the proposal team must ask more than how inventory is turned over, how receivables are collected, and what type of reporting system is used. Today, many firms provide sales training for their professionals, to familiarize team members with the kinds of questions that draw out needed information. A technique commonly used is the open-ended question, which requires a fairly detailed answer, not a simple "yes" or "no." It makes the prospective client elaborate on and volunteer details—details that can give you the winning edge. Examples of open-ended questions are: "What do you think are the biggest challenges facing you today—both personally and for the company?" "Why do you think so?" "Could you describe the process for selecting a new accounting firm?" "What would happen if you were to change your year end to August 31st?"

It is helpful to form a list of questions to use during the site visit. The list should include all questions furnished to the prospective client in advance, plus any additional questions not included with the introductory letter.

It is a good idea for at least one proposal team member to have this list of questions with him or her at the site visit. This list will prompt the proposal team in their questioning and ensure that no questions are overlooked. In addition, it provides an organized method for recording the prospective client's responses, including any unusual or casual comments. Try listing the questions on the left side of the page with the corresponding answers on the right.

Exhibit 3.3 provides sample questions to be asked during a site visit.

Exhibit 3.3   *Sample Questions for a Site Visit*

Technical Information

1. To what extent and in what areas can we rely on your existing internal audit staff to support us?

2. What do you think are the most critical areas of risk in your business? How can you limit your exposure?

3. What information can you provide that will help us to obtain a basic understanding of your operations and activities for planning the audit?

4. Are your internal reporting systems functioning as effectively as you think they could? What are their strengths and weaknesses?

5. Do you anticipate any other changes in the financial area in the next year? How could those changes affect the selection of a new auditor?

6. Do you use the LIFO, FIFO, or weighted-average inventory method? Why is the one used the best for your operations?

7. Do you anticipate any manufacturing or systems changes in the near future? What kind of impact do you expect them to have on the organization?

8. How are your overseas financial operations managed? Do you anticipate any problems or changes in the near future?

Personnel-Related Information

9. What kinds of changes have you made in company-wide staffing in the past year? Why? Do you anticipate more?

10. Do you anticipate any changes in your internal audit or tax staffing in the coming year?

Issues/Needs/Goals

11. What do you think will have the biggest impact on your industry and your company over the next five years? Why?

12. How have you prepared for this effect?

13. Is the transition to a new auditor a concern for you? Why? What could we do to lessen your concern?

14. Do you have a formal corporate goals or mission statement? Is it effective? Why or why not?

Relationships/Communications

15. What kind of working relationship do you and senior management prefer to have with your auditors? Have you had it in the past?

16. Would you like to meet periodically with our firm's top industry specialist? How often?

(Continued on next page.)

Exhibit 3.3   *Sample Questions for a Site Visit (Continued)*

17. How frequently and in what forms do you prefer to receive communications from your auditors? Do your current auditors communicate in this manner?

18. How could we work best with your audit committee?

19. If you could change three things about your current audit or audit firm, what would they be?

Selection Criteria

20. What do you think are the most important criteria your management should consider in selecting a CPA firm? Why?

21. Which members of your company do you expect to participate in the decision/selection process? Why were they chosen? [Even if you know the answer to this question, you should ask it. You may be surprised.]

22. Why are you choosing new auditors now?

23. Have you participated in the selection of a new auditor before? How was the process different from this one?

24. Which firm do you think has the leading edge? What would it take for our firm to win?

SITE-VISIT DEBRIEFING

Following each major site visit, the proposal team members meet as soon as possible to review what transpired and identify useful information. Sometimes even seemingly insignificant information can play a major role in the development of the proposal. To be sure that vital information is identified, have a member of your staff who did not meet the prospective client ask the proposal team the following questions:

- How would you characterize the personal style of the CEO/decision maker? What do others say about him or her?

- What were your impressions of each representative you interviewed? What words or expressions did he or she use often?

- How do you think the point of view of the CEO might differ from that of the CFO?

- How are decisions made in the company?

- What could we do for the prospective client (i.e., for the company or for key individuals personally) that has not been requested already?

- What will it take (fee or other commitment) to win the work? Can we give it?

- What type of management dissatisfaction or pending internal changes did you detect or suspect?

- What is the company's mission statement and its long-term goals?

- How would you describe the office working environment? How do workers dress and talk to one another? Is it quiet, noisy, or formal?

- What is our probable chance of winning the engagement (5 percent, 50 percent, 90 percent)? Can we increase our chances?

Getting the Most Out of a Meeting

Certain meeting skills can help make interviews with the prospective client effective and profitable. These skills include effective listening and simple courtesy.

EFFECTIVE
LISTENING

Listening is hard work and requires discipline. The brain processes information four times faster than people speak, which means the listener is often a few steps ahead of the speaker. Unfortunately, when the listener is ahead of the conversation, he or she is likely to miss what is being said. Also, no matter how hard we try to listen to another's point of view, what we hear is still filtered through our own experiences.

Listening in proposal situations takes two forms:

1. *Listening to File.* Listening to file means listening *for* certain information, not listening *to* the speaker. You focus your attention on items you want to note for your agenda, for example, information on the prospective client's criteria for selecting a new accounting firm or on the client's long-term goals.

2. *Listening to Give.* Listening to give means listening for opportunities to deliver certain information to the prospective client. For example, you listen for a chance to mention an industry expert's credentials or your firm's most distinctive features.

Your task is to know your purpose in each meeting and to use the proper listening mode. When listening to file, do not underestimate the value of note taking. The simple act of taking careful notes during interviews serves two important purposes. First, it demonstrates interest in and respect for the prospective client's comments. Second, these notes can be invaluable when the proposal team develops the "win" strategy.

COURTESY

Good manners, in business as anywhere else, are about human relationships and choices. Here is what that means when applied to face-to-face meetings with a prospective client:

- Make a good first impression. Be on time. Greet, shake hands with, and give your card to everyone present. Be sure you note every name.

- Remain standing until invited to sit. Treat someone else's office as if it were his or her home. Ask permission before you move papers or pick up any personal item from the desk or shelves. Place your briefcase on your lap or the floor, not on the prospective client's desk.

- Clarify at the beginning of a meeting how much time the prospective client can give you and honor that timetable—even if it means you can't say everything you had planned.

- As a rule, the person who requests the meeting determines the agenda. However, even if you initiated the meeting and arrive with a prepared agenda, be courteous enough to allow the prospective client to change it.

- If it's a lunch meeting, you pay. Skip the alcoholic drinks, even if the prospective client is drinking.

Remember, courtesy does not stop when the meeting ends. If you promise anything, be sure you deliver it. When appropriate, follow up quickly with thank-you notes. And lastly, make first impressions and last words count. They are frequently what the prospective client will remember best.

Chapter 4:
The "Win" Strategy

After gathering as much information as possible about the company, its leaders, and the selection process through research and interviews, the proposal team is ready to develop its "win" strategy.

A single win strategy is ideal, but committing yourself to one specific strategy is risky for two reasons. First, the wrong decision can mean losing the engagement; second, later developments may cause the proposal team to modify or change its strategy. That is no doubt why proposal teams often try to communicate as many messages as possible to the prospective client. Unfortunately, this approach can dilute the most important message that can be communicated—that you understand the prospective client's specific needs.

Analyze the Information Gathered

Win strategy development begins with a systematic analysis of the needs and concerns expressed or implied by the prospective client and other sources.

Your goal in this analysis is to distill the criteria the prospective client will use for selecting its new accountants. The body of research into the categories companies use to define what they want from their accountants may be condensed into the "twelve C's," which answer the question, "Why do companies select a particular accounting firm?" By focusing on these twelve influencing factors, you focus your strategy accurately to reflect the weight of the prospective client's selection criteria. The twelve C's are as follows:

1. Cost—Is their fee in the acceptable range?

2. Chemistry—Do they like and trust us?

3. Comparable experience— For whom have they handled similar issues?

4. Capabilities—Do they have the trained staff and technology on hand in the right locations?

5. Credentials—Who are their other clients?

6. Clear communication—Do they tell us what we want/need to know as often as we would like in a form we like?

7. Client service commitment—How important are we to them and what do their references say?

8. Centralized control—Can the service team members manage this work effectively and efficiently?

9. Competence—Can we rely on them to do the right thing?

10. Continuity—How will they limit staff turnover?

11. Creativity/Initiative—Will they look for ideas/savings to bring to us?

12. Contacts—How well do we know members of the proposal team?

Assess which of the twelve C's the prospective client is most likely to use in its evaluation process. It frequently will be one of the following:

- Cost
- Capabilities
- Chemistry
- Comparable experience

In addition, never underestimate the importance of contacts. Contacts can make or break a proposal's success by providing information and supporting your firm as the preferred choice. It is important that the proposal team identify contacts they have within the prospective client's organization and decide how best to use those contacts. The tactics of maintaining and managing contacts should be an integral part of the proposal strategy.

Remember, your firm must accomplish two things in its proposal to a prospective client: First, it must satisfy those of the twelve C's that are important to this prospective client and second, it must distinguish itself from all other firms that also could satisfy them.

Exhibit 4.1 illustrates how the twelve C's may be used to determine each decision maker's personal needs. This proposal strategy matrix identifies, evaluates, and prioritizes the C's most important to each DMU member. To complete the chart, use comments and observations from research and interviews, as well as your own experience in similar situations. It may be helpful to prepare a summary that highlights the most important issues to guide your overall strategy. Asking the following questions for each DMU member can assist in this process:

- What does he or she want from me/us at this time?
- Can I/we provide it?
- How can I/we exceed his/her expectations?

These questions help to address each individual's goals and needs in terms of the corporate goals. Identifying the goals and needs of the DMU members can set your firm apart from competing firms and demonstrate the value your firm could bring if selected.

Exhibit 4.1   *Proposal Strategy Matrix*

Person/Executive			
Selection Criteria	*Very Important*	*Important*	*Not Important*
Cost			
Chemistry			
Comparable experience			
Capabilities			
Clear communication			
Client service commitment			
Centralized control			
Competence			
Continuity			
Creativity/Initiative			
Contacts			

Evaluate the Circumstances of a Reproposal

A request for a reproposal from an existing client can be devastating, but it is rarely unexpected. In some cases, the client is subject to regulatory policies that require mandatory auditor rotation. In most cases, the cause is one of the following: (1) management changes at the client's company, (2) dissatisfaction with the level of service provided by the current firm, or (3) dissatisfaction with current fees. By opening the door to other firms, the client is sending a message that the incumbent firm has failed to satisfy its needs or expectations. This puts the incumbent firm at a disadvantage and on the defensive. As in any relationship, it is important to show the client that you hear and understand the dissatisfaction and will take the steps necessary to correct it. Further discussion of the unique considerations of reproposals is in chapter 5.

Although the reevaluation process may involve delicate company political issues and/or painful performance reviews, the more open the firm is in addressing and repairing any breaches in the relationship with the client, the more likely it is that the proposal team will succeed with the reproposal. When reevaluating the firm's role, the proposal team—

- **Finds out why the client is requesting a reproposal.** Are there disagreements on accounting positions or procedures? Does the client want a lower fee? Has the client undergone an organizational restructuring? Is there new management? Work hard to uncover both the obvious and the less obvious reasons for the reproposal and use them as building blocks on which to construct the proposal.

- **Examines current relationships with the members of the client's DMU.** View the opportunity as a prospective new client. Identify the primary decision maker (this should be easy, unless the client's business has been restructured). Review the DMU's goals. Has its needs changed? What can be done that was not done previously to improve the client's profitability or achieve its business goals?

- **Reviews the track record critically.** Has past service been perceived as good or bad by the DMU? What about the service has been perceived as good and what has been perceived as bad?

- **Analyzes what the competition will say and do.** Have any other firms performed work for the client? How have their services been perceived by the DMU? Have they been asked to propose? What strengths are they likely to offer?

- **Reviews fee history.** Are fees appropriate for the current competitive environment? Is the client in a cost-cutting mode? Is the client aware that he or she receives full value for the fees paid?

- **Reassesses the existing service team.** Is the group ideal for the assignment? Why? Should it be changed in any way? If the group is changed, how will this be explained to the client? Will new group members bring something new that the client would like to have?

Define the Win Strategy

The strategy that dominates the rest of the proposal process is based on the proposal team's assessment of your firm's greatest advantage over its competitors in the eyes of the prospective client.

How can you identify this strategy? Both the strategy and the way you uncover it will vary from proposal to proposal. The winning strategy may come as a burst of inspiration from a single team member or it may be the consensus arrived at in a group planning session. Reviewing the selection criteria outlined in the proposal strategy matrix (presented earlier in this chapter) and asking the following questions is one way to get started.

- Are the stated needs of the prospective client genuine? Do you need to help the prospective client understand something it does not see clearly?

- What are the various ways in which each need can be satisfied (by your firm or any other)? What is the best way?

- How can you restate each need in terms of the best way to solve the problem?
- How can you help the client to understand something it does not see clearly and how can you prove that your firm has helped others to solve similar problems?

Another method of identifying your win strategy, whether for the proposal document or the oral presentation, is brainstorming. A brainstorming session enables proposal team members to focus on all comments, observations, and details. To start, have one proposal team member write down everyone's key thoughts and then organize them by issue. One approach is to use index cards, another is to use a facilitator and flip chart. Once you have a group of similar topics, generate a title that states the main idea. The next step is to reduce the number of groups until you have defined seven or fewer points.

Now look at the titles and arrange the points in order of importance *to the primary decision maker.* These groups will form the basic outline of your written proposal or oral presentation. The heading that emerges as number one in importance to the primary decision maker most likely encompasses the win strategy. If there are several issues of importance, look for the common thread that links them. That will be the win strategy.

Communicate the Win Strategy

At this point, the proposal team knows what should be said and to whom. The unresolved question is "How?" Occasionally, a prospective client has pressing needs (for example, unintegrated computer systems) that can affect your work. Educating the DMU about its actual needs can be a tricky proposition, requiring a great deal of tact, sensitivity, and intelligence. The DMU should see the proposal team as knights prepared to fight for their best interests, not as teachers lecturing on the company's inadequacies. There are several ways to help the proposal team members focus on their strategy and convey their selling messages. These include—

- Focusing on key words.
- Adapting the presentation style.
- Highlighting the benefits.
- Being persuasive.

Any of these methods can be used effectively in both the proposal document and the oral presentation.

FOCUS ON KEY WORDS

After establishing your strategy, it is useful to find key words that can articulate the strategy and reinforce your principal message to the DMU.

Some firms have used slogans to help convey a theme or image in their proposals. They include such phrases as:

- All the strength you need for your bottom line
- [*Your firm's name*] and [*the prospective client's company name*]—a winning combination
- Partners in progress
- Aggressive actions require quick decisions

The slogan can also be a key word, for example:

- Quality
- Cost effective
- Superior client service
- Partnership

A slogan can reflect many things about your firm or your team. It can reflect a purpose, work ethic, or public image, or an approach to the work required by the prospective client. Teams that use a slogan to prepare their proposal document or oral presentation often find that the document and presentation are more focused and clear—both for the proposal team and for the audience.

ADAPT THE PRESENTATION STYLE

Convincing DMU members that your firm knows what they want and that it can deliver is the essence of the proposal communication. This may mean varying the way you normally present your credentials or represent the firm. It is the job of each proposal team to tailor all communications so that each DMU member gets the information needed to make a decision in a way that is natural and easy. To be persuasive, the presenters must adapt their own preferred style to the style most appropriate for each opportunity.

It is important that good chemistry exist between members of the proposal team and the DMU, particularly the primary decision maker. To create good chemistry, first consider how the primary decision maker's preferences, styles, and needs may differ from your own or those of your team, and alter your delivery of information accordingly. The following are some sample situations and appropriate responses.

- The key decision maker is a directorial, bottom-line kind of person who doesn't want to be bothered with a lot of details.

  — Get right to the point in writing and use a lot of bullet points. Ask for a quick decision.

- The key decision maker wants to draw his or her own conclusion based on careful evaluation of the facts.

  — Provide not only the background details, but also any important justifications for selecting your firm. Expect a slow decision.

- The primary decision maker is very reserved.

— Don't try to do business over a beer at the local hangout or ask a lot of personal questions about his or her family or interests. Keep the conversation on business matters.

- The primary decision maker is very open and outgoing.

— Be cheerful, stimulating, and informal. Tell personal anecdotes.

The goal is to adapt your own natural communication style to more closely match that of the primary decision maker. This does not mean adopting a false personality. You simply want the primary decision maker and the DMU to see you as a person who can fit into the company's organizational culture and style. To fit in, it is your job to adapt your natural style so that others see it as compatible with theirs.

HIGHLIGHT THE BENEFITS

Most proposal team members know that, in addition to describing the firm and its services, they must also highlight the benefits of these services in order to win. However, identifying benefits is a challenge for most people, and it is where proposals most often fail. To take this extra step, proposal team members must understand and articulate the difference between features and benefits.

A *feature* is a service or expertise a firm can provide. When the proposal team tells a prospective client about the services or expertise the firm offers (such as tax consulting, a software program, or a well trained staff), it is talking about features.

A *benefit* is what the client gains *as a result* of using the service or expertise. When the proposal team talks about what the company will receive as a result of using that service or expertise (for example, money or time saved, credibility, or staff efficiency), it is offering benefits.

Benefits strongly influence the sale, but they are sometimes difficult to define. One effective method to identify benefits is to answer the question, "What will the prospective client *be, do, gain,* or *save* as a result of this feature or service?"

In addition to the benefits to the prospective client's company, the proposal team should also focus on the benefits to the individual members of the DMU. Identifying clearly the benefits the individual executives will receive as a result of your service or expertise is the extra step that can answer the unspoken question "What's in it for me" and win over your audience.

Asking what the prospective client will be, do, gain, or save prevents the common error of confusing a feature or service with its benefit. The following are some examples that demonstrate what a person or company can be, do, gain, and save.

•	Be—	Up-to-date	Visible	Effective
		Efficient	Influential	An authority
		Competitive	Decisive	Creative
•	Do—	Meet goals	Fulfill obligations	Satisfy curiosity
		Win approval	Evidence care	
		Establish a precedent	Resist domination	
•	Gain—	Time	Money	Support
		Recognition	Praise	Trust
		Approval	Security	Advancement
•	Save—	Work	Time	Money
		Risks	Credibility	Jobs
		Money	Worry	

Ask this question for each feature and service identified in the proposal strategy matrix. Remember that while the win strategy helps the proposal team focus on the primary decision maker's main concerns, there are other members of the DMU whose concerns must also be addressed. The proposal team's goal is to appeal to every individual's specific needs and concerns, and then to communicate persuasively in both the proposal document and the oral presentation.

BE PERSUASIVE

Proposals are persuasive communications and a proposal must persuade to succeed. But people resist change. In order to overcome resistance to change, the proposal team must persuade the DMU members that it can solve or reduce their current problems. To do that, it must tactfully confront the DMU with the issues that have led up to this proposal and then convince them of how they can benefit from making the change to your firm.

A number of things can be done to ensure that the proposal document and oral presentation both persuade and inform.

1. *Prove it.* Claims of what the proposal team can do to help the prospective client are hollow unless examples are given of how your firm has helped others in similar situations. Proof is one of the strongest persuaders. No client wants service providers to learn at its expense. If your firm has performed the service before, say so. And be specific. In most cases, you can name clients, and you should always provide the results or outcome. Proof is evidence: examples, experiences, or expert testimony.

2. *Focus on the issues that have given rise to the change of firms.* Remind the DMU of the problems that have resulted in its current problems, and hold out a promise of a solution.

3. *Demonstrate added value.* Added value is that extra something received over and above what is actually paid for. It is the extra something that the proposal team does that exceeds the DMU's expectations. In the case of an audit, added value may include the continuity provided by the audit staff during a

period of high employee turnover for the prospective client. Or it could be the firm's industry experts watching over the shoulders of the audit staff and making recommendations about how management could improve other areas of the company's operations.

4. *Show that your firm is better equipped than the competition.* Be aware of what services and features competing firms will offer to the prospective client. Offset or neutralize any advantage they may have by citing a comparable advantage of using your firm. Point out why that advantage is relevant to the prospective client and why your firm provides it better.

Chapter 5:
The Proposal Document

The proposal document is the first point in the proposal process where all the proposal team's research, analysis, and strategic planning come together. As shown in the proposal process outline in chapter 1, the proposal document is only one of several factors influencing the prospective client's selection, but it is a crucial one. It is the image of the firm on paper. Although the proposal document alone usually does not win the engagement for a firm, it can easily be the reason that a firm is eliminated from further consideration.

The proposal document tells the prospective client—

- How well the firm understands the needs and expectations of both the organization as a whole and the individual members of management.

- How the firm meets the prospective client's selection/decision criteria.

- How the firm differs from the competition.

- How professional the firm is.

- How committed the firm is.

- How well qualified the firm's team is to do the work needed.

- The estimated fees the firm will charge to do the work needed.

Parts of the Proposal Document

There are four typical parts to a proposal document: the transmittal letter, the executive summary, the body, and the appendixes. Not all parts appear in every type of proposal document. Therefore, each part in its own way stresses the benefits the prospective client will receive as a result of the firm's services and features. The entire proposal document must reflect the win strategy.

THE TRANSMITTAL LETTER

The transmittal letter can take two forms. It can act as an executive summary highlighting the key selling points of the proposal, or it can be a brief introductory letter that drives home your primary message, with a separate executive summary attachment. Regardless of the form, the transmittal letter is an important opportunity to reflect the strategy of the proposal document. The transmittal letter expresses and emphasizes—

- The firm's appreciation at being considered.
- The firm's understanding of the reasons for the RFP.
- The firm's understanding of the nature of the project or engagement.
- The experience/expertise of the service team.
- The primary reason why your firm is best qualified to perform the required services.
- A sincere desire to work with the prospective client on this project.
- Enthusiasm.

Last, but most important, the transmittal letter is where the proposal team asks for the business. Sometimes, professional service firms present their credentials without expressing their eagerness to do the work. They assume this is something the prospective client knows. But if the proposal team never asks for the work, it may be awarded to a firm that appears more interested.

THE EXECUTIVE SUMMARY

In proposal documents that are thirty pages or longer (including appendixes), it is appropriate to include a brief executive summary. This summary highlights your points of difference and key selling messages. It should be two pages or less. The executive summary does not need to follow any predefined sequence or format. It should be structured any way that makes sense for the primary decision maker. It does not have to mirror the proposal document, which may have a different audience.

The executive summary can be arranged graphically in a table, in parallel columns, in an interview format, or in simple, short paragraphs with headlines that convey your selling messages.

THE BODY

If a detailed, structured outline is given in the RFP, the proposal team normally should follow it carefully. If the proposal team chooses not to answer a specific question, it should acknowledge and explain the omission. Recently, some firms have elected to organize all their proposals in order of importance and add a cross-reference page, based on the RFP, that tells the prospective client where to find needed information. This is usually acceptable, unless the prospective client has requested the firm to follow the RFP structure.

When there is no outline provided in the RFP, the proposal team is free to present the information in any format it chooses. In such cases, the issues identified in the brainstorming session (described in chapter 4) become the body of the proposal document and the weight given to those issues determines the order in which they are presented. The proposal team should not be swayed from the sequence arrived at in the brainstorming session unless there is new information or the overall strategy changes.

Once the key issues and their proper sequence have been determined, the proposal team can construct a persuasive proposal document. The proposal team can do this by—

- Relating each key issue to a benchmark within the prospective client's industry. (For example, if the issue for a hospital is third-party reimbursements, relate its reimbursement rate to the average reimbursement rate for other hospitals of comparable size around the country.)

- Making a specific recommendation and then giving examples of how the firm has helped other clients save money, improve processes, or expand capabilities in similar circumstances.

This kind of proposal structure will set the firm apart from the rest of the pack by demonstrating both an understanding of the prospective client's business (gained through listening) and a knowledge of the industry.

All unsubstantiated claims must be avoided (for example, avoid phrases like "We are uniquely qualified to . . ." and "We are the leading . . ."). Any claim should be backed up with proof that supports the claim. This gives the firm much greater credibility with prospective clients and helps to differentiate your firm.

APPENDIXES

Using appendixes for general or boilerplate information on the firm and service team helps keep the body of the proposal focused on key issues and strategic messages. Appendixes most frequently contain two types of information: general information on the firm and other useful information not requested in the RFP.

Use appendixes to provide such information as—

- Detailed descriptions of special services and/or fees for projects beyond the primary scope of the proposal.

- Audit scope or work schedule.

- Extended descriptions of the firm, its history, special service techniques, resources, and proprietary methodologies.

- A list of firm locations or overseas personnel.

- Biographies of service team members (photos optional).

- A list of representative clients, including those in the prospective client's major industries.

- A list of firm offices that will serve the prospective client's locations (including offices of firms affiliated through firm associations).

- Copies of testimonial letters from clients.

- Firm publications and article reprints.

- References for individuals on the service team.

- Other information requested by the prospective client.

To make the appendixes effective, tailor to the prospective client even boilerplate material, such as current client lists and firm history, expertise, and resources. Don't make the DMU guess how this information is relevant to their specific needs and goals. And, if the information is generic or was not asked for specifically, consider omitting it altogether.

Types of Proposal Documents

There are four basic types of proposal documents:

1. Statement of qualifications
2. Fee proposal
3. Letter proposal
4. Reproposal

The RFP and discussions with the prospective client indicate which type is required. Descriptions of each type of written proposal follow with examples of information that can be included; sample proposals documents are in appendix C.

STATEMENT OF QUALIFICATIONS

Statements of qualifications or statements of credentials are typically requested by organizations that have not yet made a commitment to change accounting firms, but want to assess their options in the marketplace. Sometimes a statement of qualifications request is a company's method of alerting its current provider that a higher level of service or a lower fee is desired to continue the relationship. When a statement of qualifications is requested, the possibility always exists that no change of accountants will be made at this time. However, requests for statements of qualifications often lead to a fee proposal opportunity within the following twelve months, particularly when the prospective client discovers that other firms are interested and could potentially provide better service, a new perspective, or a lower fee.

Successful proposal teams find ways to make even routine statements of qualifications persuasive and compelling. They also put a program in place to ensure that the prospective client has many opportunities to meet and socialize with the firm's partners and industry experts throughout the coming year. A statement of qualifications often contains the following:

1. Transmittal letter
2. Body
   - National/worldwide credentials, or affiliations with other firms
   - Local office credentials, such as staff head count in a particular industry
   - A service team organization chart
   - Specific industry credentials and credentials of the lead partner

- Description of the expertise of relevant industry specialists
- Specific firm issues important to the prospective client (such as litigation record, peer review, client gains/losses, continuing education of staff, head count statistics)
- Charts and graphs that show your standing or market share in the industry (for example, your clients in the *Fortune* 500, *Inc.* 100, *Forbes* multinationals, local business journal's top 25, *Crain's New York Business*, etc.)
- Quotes from relevant newspapers, books, or clients about your firm's expertise (only if recent and significant)

3. Appendixes

FEE PROPOSAL

A fee proposal answers the prospective client's question, "Can we afford you?" This type of proposal document is most common, except in states where quoting fee estimates is not allowed. In a fee proposal, some firms provide most of the necessary information in a few paragraphs or pages. Larger firms, however, typically devote whole chapters to each topic when proposing to a major prospective client.

There are two possible fee proposal situations. In the first, the prospective client has previously requested and reviewed your firm's statement of qualifications and is now ready to discuss the bottom line. In the second, the prospective client has not seen your firm's qualifications in writing, and is interested in hearing not only about your firm, but also about fees.

When a statement of qualifications has recently been provided, the fee proposal is brief and does not repeat the same material. It contains only a reminder of those key selling points that highlight the firm's strengths and, of course, the fee estimate. In this situation, the fee proposal usually contains the following:

1. Transmittal letter
2. Executive summary
3. Body
   - Brief review of the key points of distinction
   - Fees and services to be provided for the fees quoted
   - Client testimonials (quotes or letters of recommendation)

In situations where no statement of qualifications was requested prior to the fee proposal, the fee proposal document may resemble a statement of qualifications with a fee section added.

LETTER PROPOSAL

Most smaller firms use the equivalent of a standardized form letter for many proposal opportunities. Because these firms are generally working with smaller or family-owned businesses, a short, personal proposal is appropriate. Additionally, the proposal team may have had the benefit of discussing the typical elements of a proposal document in earlier face-to-face meetings with management.

Letter proposals are typically four to seven pages long. They are effective because they are brief. The prospective client usually reads every word, which may not be the case with larger proposal documents.

Short proposals can be more challenging to write than larger proposals, because they must focus immediately on the key issues. There is no room for wordiness or antiquated formalities. Letter proposals may include the following:

1. Body
   - Introductory paragraph
   - Observations of the prospective client's needs and recommendations
   - Short team biographies (stating why each person's experience is relevant to this prospect)
   - Statement of why your firm is better suited to serve the prospect than any other firm
   - Services to be rendered and how they will benefit the prospective client
   - Fee
   - Description of how your firm has helped others in similar circumstances
2. Appendixes

No matter how small your firm or how small the prospective client, the letter proposal should be prepared as carefully as a lengthy written proposal for a major prospective client.

REPROPOSAL

No one likes to be told that he or she is performing poorly. Since that is a common reason for soliciting a proposal, reproposals or retention proposals are often the most difficult to prepare. In order to retain the client, the team must—

- Make an honest appraisal of the situation and, if appropriate, acknowledge that errors have been made and describe all changes that will ensue.

- Emphasize what the firm has done for the client in the past and why those services were important. (This is crucial if there has been a recent management change.)

- Emphasize the disruption and loss of experience that would result from a change of firms.

- Highlight the benefits of the firm's involvement in the client's future.

If the reproposal is a result of management changes, spend time documenting the history of the firm's participation, achievements, and concern for the client's best interests. Don't assume that the new management knows these things. Include concrete examples of accomplishments, dollars saved (where possible), and justifications for the approach taken in the work (in case the new management favors another approach). Express willingness to adopt new procedures and help hold down costs, a certain concern of every new executive.

The reproposal document typically contains these elements:

1. Transmittal letter, outlining your track record and the savings or benefits your firm has provided the client

2. Executive summary, outlining changes that will be made, if any (for example, a new lead partner, a guarantee of staff continuity above the senior level for the next three years, or a reduced fee)

3. Body
   - A service team organization chart describing team changes to be made in response to client needs/requests (or emphasizing continuity if personnel problems were not part of the reason for the reproposal)
   - Discussion of why continuing with your firm is in the best interest of the client
   - Brief biographies of any new service team members, including reasons for the changes (i.e., what the new people will bring that the current team lacks)
   - Detailed discussion of your past efforts on behalf of the client and the benefits or savings the client has received (for example, case studies of how you have helped the client save money or work through a difficult time)
   - Predictions of how your firm will be instrumental in helping the client with upcoming deals or situations of which competing firms may not be aware
   - Fees, including explanations for any reductions offered (for example, new technology or revised scope)

4. Appendixes

Fee Presentation in the Proposal Document

Normally, the first time the prospective client is presented with estimated fees is in the proposal document. Fee presentation in the proposal document is therefore very important. There are numerous issues for the proposal team to consider when presenting fees, such as the total fee, hourly rate, "freebies," premium rates, and fee justification in reproposals. Samples of fee presentations are included in appendix D.

GENERAL GUIDELINES

In general, present all fee estimates in a confident and nondefensive way. Don't apologize for your fee before you state it. Tell the prospective client exactly how and when the fees are payable, when fees might be reviewed, and the terms for specialists' services (if appropriate).

Don't feel obligated to provide all information related to fees (for example, a table of hours by staff level or billing rates by staff level). Say only what is necessary. Be sure the prospective client knows that the fee or range quoted is an estimate that can be fine-tuned through further discussion. If the prospective client is encouraged to come back for clarification or explanation of the fee presentation, the proposal team will have an opportunity to negotiate and overcome objections of which it might not otherwise have been aware.

If the fees quoted are considerably different from those charged by the incumbent firm, the firm could be asked to explain the difference. For this reason, the proposal team should document the approach and rationale used in determining the fee quote.

HOURLY RATES

Larger firms are often reluctant to provide hourly fees charged for various levels of personnel. Some have formal policies covering fee quotes for work to be performed. They often prefer to provide a flat rate (or range) for the entire audit plus out-of-pocket expenses, and then absorb any cost overruns. If pressed for specific breakdowns, these firms may provide rates in the form of a fee range per hour per level of staff. This allows them the flexibility to bill at rates suited to the level of work performed.

Smaller firms can be more aggressive. They rightly perceive their lower rates to be a competitive advantage over larger firms. Smaller firms often approach fees candidly by stating precisely what their hourly rates are for each level of staff. Divulging fixed hourly rates presents a potential problem, however, and should be done carefully, especially in smaller communities. The prospective client may reveal the rates to other clients of the firm that are charged a different rate, creating an awkward situation that could result in the loss of a client.

If a proposal team elects to present its hourly fee rates, quoting an hourly fee range for each staff level is a useful option. The proposal team can justify this on the grounds that it provides flexibility and allows the lead partner to use professional judgment in selecting the appropriate level of staff for the work required.

To help the prospective client make a fair comparison of fees, encourage a comparison based on the estimated number of audit hours. This ensures an apples-to-apples comparison and gets the audit price calculated at the lowest number of hours. Treat any other work separately for fee estimation purposes, even if it is within the scope of the proposal.

"FREEBIES"

Several years ago, proposing to absorb all start-up costs was likely to be considered an aggressive approach. Today, it is common practice. Businesses expect firms to absorb start-up costs as part of the cost of doing business. When drafting the proposal document, the proposal team should keep in mind that it will probably impress the prospective client more if a dollar value is attached to the start-up investment.

Including other services at no charge can appeal to many cost-conscious prospective clients. Very often, services that need to be performed prior to the audit can be identified and highlighted as free services. These may include studies or reviews in the prospective client's relevant business segments or a specialized tax analysis. To be most effective, the proposal document must clearly spell out the functional and dollar values of such services.

Freebies also provide an excellent opportunity for management advisory or tax consultants to get to know the client; they frequently also reveal extra work the firm can perform for additional fees. Just remember that, to be worthwhile, any freebie must have immediate perceived value to the prospective client and, once performed, should lead to the possibility of additional work for the firm.

PREMIUM RATES

Every prospective client has a fee range it considers acceptable. If the economics of the practice require that your firm's fees be high, the proposal team must take special care to emphasize and justify the added value the prospective client receives for paying a higher fee. Many companies will pay the high end of the range if they believe they will receive more.

Value is what we gain over and above what we expected to receive for what we paid. To show added value, discourage the prospective client from comparisons of fee scales or rates and chargeable hours. Instead, highlight the value received for money paid. It is not always an easy task for most firms to identify or highlight the added value they will give a client. It can involve a change in thinking to—

- Identify the services or features that differentiate your firm from any other (for example, providing a unique industry service or having a former commissioner of the IRS on your staff).

- Identify those extras that matter to the prospective client and that he or she gains as a result of using your firm (for example, greater hands-on participation by an experienced lead partner or additional staff resources available during peak busy periods).

- Explain why the prospective client should be willing to pay more to receive such extras (for example, peace of mind or shareholder confidence).

REPROPOSALS

In a reproposal, the proposal team must address the fee history and either justify the current fee level or provide a plausible explanation for a proposed reduction.

If, in order to save a client, the fee must be lowered, try the following approaches: show value for money, unbundle any extra services previously provided as part of your services, and demonstrate economies of scale, if applicable.

Demonstrate That Experience Pays

The incumbent firm has invested significant time and has a track record of achievement in the client's business. Let the proposal prove this by demonstrating that the firm's staff is already familiar with the client's personnel, routines, reporting procedures, systems, and business issues. As a result, the client will suffer no downtime caused by transition to a new firm. The firm's partners have also worked with top management to find ways to help it achieve its goals (cite examples of this). And show that the firm's personnel have good working relationships with the client's personnel and that the two groups complement each other and know how to work well together. Use names of client personnel and cite examples of work done over the years to accomplish the client's goals. These are huge advantages for which the client should be willing to pay more than the lowest fee proposed.

Show the True Cost of the Audit

When the client hired the firm originally, it was to perform a specific task, for example, a statutory audit. The job may have included certain extra work or an approach that is no longer necessary, or there may have been client inefficiencies that had to be remedied. One constructive approach to a new fee quote is to remind the client of the additional work that was originally reflected in the firm's fee and why that work was needed. Explain to the client that the additional services are no longer required and that new, lower fees pertain only to the audit. If extra services must be included in the audit fee, cost out those services separately from the new, lower fee quote. This method provides a legitimate way for the client to make an apples-to-apples comparison.

Introduce New Technology

Another alternative is to justify fee reductions on the basis of economies of scale or technology advances. For example, the firm may now be using computerized audit procedures or doing technical research on a CD-ROM computer disk instead of in library stacks. Such streamlining saves time and represents savings that the firm can pass along to the client in the form of new, lower fees. Of course, this raises the question of why the firm failed to pass those savings on to the client before! Be sure to advise the client that the savings are due to new technology that was only recently brought on line.

Draft the Proposal Document

Once the proposal team has determined the strategy, content, and form of the proposal document, all that is left to do is to sit down and write it. Some basic guidelines for producing an effective proposal document include the following:

- Create an outline. Start by outlining the chapters of the proposal document and then outline the sections in each chapter. Make the outline as detailed and as complete as possible. Using outlines can streamline the proposal writing process, reduce duplicated effort, permit centralized control, and increase effectiveness.

- When possible, avoid acronyms, abbreviations, colloquialisms, and accounting firm jargon (e.g., SPU, MAS, area partner, OMP, engagement). To the extent possible, use vocabulary from the prospective client's business and industry; otherwise, use simple English.

- Use the active voice and conversational language throughout. The writing should be like your speech—personal and readable, but businesslike without being stuffy.
- Use graphics and visual enhancements that help emphasize key points. Avoid saying in words what you present in a graphic. Place exhibits, charts, or graphs in the text as near to the reference as possible. (For lengthy lists, biographies, or references, use an appendix.)
- Each section or topic and any major subsections should contain a graphic element (table, chart, graph, or photograph) or an illustration of a complex idea discussed in that section.
- No section of the main body of the proposal should be more than three times the length of any other section (excluding the fee section, which is typically brief).
- Vary sentence length. Three typed lines should be the maximum.
- Limit lists (except client lists) to six to nine items.
- Make the proposal document skimmable. Use headlines that convey a message and bullet points to set off options, items, or observations.

While the proposal team commonly uses past proposals as a starting point, it must approach each proposal document with a fresh point of view. It is always possible to improve on what has been done before. Just because a previous proposal helped win an engagement doesn't mean that it was necessarily a good one, and just because another proposal lost doesn't make it a worthless one. Use whatever is effective wherever it comes from.

PROFESSIONAL WRITERS

Any firm able to translate its observations, approach, and suggestions into a concise, friendly, and persuasive document always has a leg up on the competition. A firm that believes it could use help in accomplishing this may want to consider using a professional writer.

There are several advantages to using a professional writer when writing the proposal document:

1. A professional writer can save money. Proposal documents can consume many labor hours of unbillable time. A professional writer, by minimizing partner and manager time, can actually pay for him- or herself many times over.

2. A professional writer can bring a new perspective and help the team focus critically on issues it may not have pinpointed previously. Also, if the proposal team's strategy and thinking is unclear, a professional writer can force the team to clarify and focus its ideas.

3. A professional writer leaves the proposal team members free to focus on interacting with the prospective client's management or on other clients—a more productive use of their time.

The expense of hiring a professional writer can be much lower than expected. In smaller towns, professional writers may charge about $25 to $50 per hour, depending on their level of experience. In larger cities, the rate may be $60 to $100 per hour. The more experienced the writer, the better value they bring.

To be effective, the professional writer must spend an hour or two interviewing key proposal team members to identify the needs and concerns of the prospective client and the key points to include in the proposal document. For this reason, a former journalist may be best. It is a myth that an outsider cannot possibly know your firm well enough to write an effective proposal. A good business communicator knows how to uncover the relevant ideas and place the emphasis accordingly.

REVIEWS

Comments of reviewers can be helpful. However, time must be allotted in the production schedule for reviews. To avoid costly and frantic last-minute changes, make every effort to have proposal document drafts reviewed early.

If the firm is large enough, it may wish to designate a proposal evaluation committee to critique all major proposal documents. The proposal team may be helped by sending a letter to reviewers requesting a critique of the proposal document along with a checklist that guides and records their responses. Exhibits 5.1 and 5.2 illustrate such a letter and sample questions that could be included.

Exhibit 5.1

Critique Request

Dear Reviewer,

Please read the attached draft of our proposal to _____
_____ and give
us your comments by _____ . Return this draft
and evaluation form to _____ .

I have also attached some information about the situation and our strategy so that you can better understand our approach, our concerns, and the prospect's concerns.

Thank you for your candid comments. Although we may not be able to use every comment from each reviewer, your observations will help us to do the best job we can.

Partner _____   Tel. No. _____

Exhibit 5.2   *Sample Questions for Proposal Evaluation Checklist*

(For Use by Reviewers)
[Note: Grade each item A, B, C, D, or F]

Does the proposal communicate—

_____   A sense of our competence, intelligence, skill, and vigor?

_____   A service philosophy and commitment that inspires confidence and trust?

_____   A sense of genuine pride in what is being presented?

_____   Our knowledge and understanding of (or willingness to learn) the essence and uniqueness of the prospective client's business and/or industry?

_____   Evidence that we did our homework—a familiarity with the business and an understanding of the nature of the problem, situation, or need that may require our attention?

_____   Evidence that we have listened to what the prospective client has told us?

_____   Persuasive arguments for our ability to adapt our service and capabilities to meet the prospective client's wants and needs?

_____   A clearly defined commitment to organization, methodology, and timing?

_____   An unmistakable relationship between service, quality, benefits, and value and proposed fees?

_____   Basic information about our firm, showing that we have the expertise, facilities, resources, experience, and track record to serve this prospect best? Such information includes—

• Our reputation for commitment to good client service and high-quality work.

• The size and nature of our practice.

• Our personnel (local and national).

• Relevant backgrounds of team personnel.

• The structure of our firm, our office, and our service delivery system.

• The relevant history of our firm.

• The relevant experience, special expertise, resources, and clientele of the office and our firm.

_____   A straightforward outline of costs, rates, fees, expenses, and billing arrangements, as appropriate?

_____   Subtle suggestions about how the decision on candidate firms might be made most effectively?

(Continued on next page.)

Exhibit 5.2   *Sample Questions for Proposal Evaluation Checklist (Continued)*

_____ A sense of our sincere desire—not just our willingness—to be selected and to serve?

_____ An emphasis on special qualities, expertise, or attributes that differentiate us from the competition?

_____ Subtle rebuttals to our competition's perceived selling strengths?

_____ The value and benefits the prospective client will receive both in general and in terms of specific attributes or services?

_____ A commitment to responsive service?

_____ A desire to develop strong relationships with key personnel in the prospective client's organization (or demonstrations of how we have done that in the past)?

_____ Information regarding specific deliverables or results the prospect can expect?

_____ A central theme for the value and benefits of our service reflecting the essence of the prospective client's needs?

_____ Our strengths and why we are best for this job?

_____ A sense that service team members were chosen specifically for their ability to do this work effectively?

Summary

_____ On a scale of 1 to 10 (10 being the best), how effective overall would you rate this proposal?

_____ Did we distinguish ourselves from all other firms?

_____ Would the proposal persuade you to choose our firm?

_____ Do you have any suggestions?

Ideally, the proposal draft in its early stages should be distributed widely to reviewers, together with a brief written summary of your strategy considerations. The number of reviewers should decrease with every draft until only one or two key people sign off on the final version.

Select the Publication Format

Different firms have different traditions of making proposals. There is no one best way. The critical issue in producing the proposal document is determining the right format and content for *this* set of decision makers at *this* time. It can be helpful to use a firm alumnus or other friendly contact within the prospective client's organization (if available) to confirm what would be the most appropriate way to present the material.

Because most larger firms have middle market and small business divisions, smaller firms can expect increasingly to find themselves competing against them head to head. To compete effectively, it may be necessary for the smaller firm to consider investments in proposal packaging.

DESKTOP PUBLISHING

Desktop publishing need not be amateurish. Sophisticated page-layout programs can turn a word-processed manuscript into an attractive and readable document in a very short time. These programs run on microcomputers and may be relatively inexpensive. Used with a laser printer, they produce high-quality pages. They can even produce a file that a service bureau will typeset, producing the highest-quality appearance. Some of the more well-known word processing software packages also have excellent layout capabilities.

The quality that desktop publishing technology provides is determined by the skill of the individual who does the work and the output device used to print the final copy. If you are training someone who has no graphics background to use the system, first invest in a desktop publishing consultant to set up tailor-made formats the firm can use for its various activities. Also, it's a good idea to get some professional guidance on selecting appropriate and compatible software packages.

Since the cost of producing a typeset document is high—especially when there are numerous revisions—it is possible that the firm can pay the entire cost of a desktop publishing system from the savings on just one or two professionally typeset projects.

PRINTING

Printing is often a hidden cost of producing higher-quality proposal documents. Midsize and larger firms frequently have their own in-house printing departments, but smaller firms rarely do—anything that they can't produce on a photocopy machine must be sent to a professional printer. This can be a significant expense, especially with rush jobs. Many printers can guarantee same-day delivery and around-the-clock service for proposal documents at a premium price, often 200 percent of the cost. In some cases, however, such expenses may be justified.

GRAPHIC DESIGN

Graphic design is more than the simple execution of organization charts and bar graphs. Today, the value a designer brings lies in interpreting qualitative information and representing it graphically in order to reduce the number of words needed in the proposal document. It is actually information design—inventing visuals that help the reader to gain knowledge and that convey essential information clearly.

Designers

A smaller firm might effectively use a graphic designer for proposals in the following ways:

- To design a standard proposal cover format (or several if the firm focuses on certain industries); this is cost effective because the covers can be printed in quantity and then overprinted (often using a photocopier) with each new prospective client's name and/or logo

- To create special proposal page layouts for the document that can then be converted to a desktop publishing format template anyone can use

- To create graphs or charts that simplify complex technical concepts and relationships

- To advise on effective and ineffective uses of logos and typefaces in proposals

- To design custom covers and layouts

Most graphic designers are moderately priced and can turn the work around quickly. Ask them to give a fee range for the work needed within the time frame required. Costs can vary greatly. For instance, a simple proposal cover, including thumbnail sketches (which are rough creative ideas), and mechanicals for reproduction can cost from $250 to $3,500. In addition to the specifications of the job, the cost is based on location, experience of the graphic designer, the proposal team's experience working with a graphic designer, and time frame. Novice freelance designers may charge $20 to $40 per hour in smaller towns and $50 to $75 per hour or more in large cities. More experienced designers, or those in advertising or public relations firms, may charge significantly more. Less experienced designers developing portfolios often charge modest fees. If the proposal team has not worked with a designer before, the designer will spend extra time educating the inexperienced team and will expect a fee at the top end of the range.

Small firms can obtain the names of reasonably priced designers by talking to art instructors at local colleges or to local nonprofit organizations that often use low-cost communications professionals to develop their materials. Be sure to ask for references and to view examples of their work. One word of caution: If the proposal team is not experienced in working with a designer, hire an experienced one. It may cost a little more, but you can be more confident that the results will meet the actual need.

Graphic Standards

Many firms have formalized graphic standards or guidelines for producing all brochures, newsletters, letters, business cards, or other materials that present an image of the firm to the public. Design proposal document formats and covers with the firm's guidelines in mind. In midsize or larger firms, check with your headquarters or national office marketing staff. If the firm doesn't have firm-wide guidelines, give the graphic designer samples of all the publications the potential client will see so the designer can create a look in harmony with those publications.

A word about type fonts and type styles. Most word processors and secretaries who use the desktop publishing capabilities present in many word-processing software packages are unschooled in the basics of graphic design and marketing communications. Their best attempts at preparing a well-designed document can cause the firm to look less than professional. To avoid this, use only one simple type font (not a script or italic font) in an easy-to-read size throughout the body of the document. Heads and subheads can be made bold-face, italic, or larger. Avoid all underscores. If certain staff are regularly responsible for producing proposals, send them for professional training in desktop graphic design.

Layout

Use page formats and spacing that enhance the readability of the document. The goal of the proposal team must always be a layout that is appropriate for the prospective client, not one that takes advantage of a new technique or technical capability that someone on the team wants to try.

Narrower columns, such as those used in a two-column format, are much easier to read and comprehend than full-page columns. Since areas of white space on the page make for easier skimming, reading, and retention, use wide margins on all sides, plenty of white space around graphics or photos, and extra space between paragraphs.

Unless you have an experienced communications professional in your office, stick with the tried and true. It works.

COLOR

Readership studies have shown that adding a second color to black-and-white text greatly increases retention of what is read. Color can be used effectively for—

- Logos.
- Headings and subheadings.
- Rules or lines on the text pages.
- Tint boxes or highlighted blocks of text.
- Graphs or charts.
- Illustrations.

Most firms prefer to reproduce proposal documents in their offices on their own copy machines. Adding a second color often means sending the document out to a printer and increasing production costs.

One way to use color cost-effectively is to have the printer preprint blank pages with one or two elements in color, such as your logo or a repeating column rule. These printed sheets can then be run through a laser copier in the office, with the black text and page numbers added.

In general, it is better to print the body text of the proposal document in black ink on white, cream, or light-grey paper. Avoid colored or heavily textured papers.

PHOTOGRAPHS

The most common photos used in proposals are head-and-shoulder publicity shots of partners and managers placed with their biographies. Some firms use photos of their office facilities or even of the prospective client's building or facilities. Most small firms do not use photographs in their proposals. However, for firms that use desktop publishing, it is easier than ever before to incorporate photographs into proposals. Here are three popular ways to process photographs and use them in proposal documents:

1. Use a grey-scale scanner that digitizes the image into a computer graphics file that can be reproduced by the computer directly onto the printed page in the same way as it does text.

2. Have a printer make velox prints from the photographs. The veloxes are pasted down on the final page layout and reproduced using an inexpensive offset printing press or even a photocopier. The charge for each velox print is about $10 to $15, depending on the printer.

3. Large print shops can use a photographic film process to reproduce photos. This method provides the clearest reproduction but is also prohibitively expensive for most smaller firms to use in proposals.

Photos add graphic interest to the proposal document and remind the DMU of the individuals who will be on the service team. However, they can be a substantial expense, since the office needs to have on hand professionally made duplicate photos of all partners and managers.

Stock photos are also sometimes used to represent the industries of the prospective client. Most professional photographers provide their unused photos to stock photo houses, which charge a fee for their use. Most large cities have stock houses, and some stock houses have toll-free telephone numbers. A local photographer can give you the names of stock photo houses in your region. Photos may be borrowed for one-time use for a flat fee (often in the $300 to $500 range each), or may be purchased outright for a higher fee. Individual photographers may also have suitable stock shots that they will provide for less money. Today, stock photos are also available on CD-ROM disks and can be downloaded directly to a laser printer.

Always avoid using color snapshots unless you are printing in color. These do not reproduce effectively in black-and-white and they appear fuzzy next to studio photos or even black-and-white snapshots.

CLIENT LOGOS
AND ADVERTISING
SLOGANS

Accounting firms often like to use the logo of a prospective client on the cover of their proposal or on the pages of the proposal document. Some companies, however, are extremely protective of their logos and slogans. They have precise and rigid rules about how, where, and when their logo may be used. Misusing it will be noticed by anyone in the organization who sees the proposal document. If you are planning to use the prospective client's logo or slogans, contact its advertising agency, marketing department, or customer service department. Ask for a camera-ready copy of the logo and instructions on its proper use. Your designer or printer may contact the department directly for the necessary technical specifications.

Be sure to ask the prospective client for the "PMS number" of the color so that the artist or printer can match it precisely. If it is a specially mixed color, ask if there is an acceptable PMS color to use if the special color is unavailable. A designer may be able to identify the color if you are reluctant to ask the prospective client.

Chapter 6:
The Oral Presentation

The oral presentation is never a regurgitation of the proposal document. If the proposal team has gotten this far, the firm's capabilities are presumably acceptable. The proposal team should therefore use the oral presentation as a fresh opportunity to deliver information important to the prospective client.

An invitation from the prospective client to make an oral presentation can come soon after the written proposal has been delivered or later on. Successful teams use the time between the delivery of the proposal document and the oral presentation to refine their strategy and rehearse their presentation. Occasionally, the prospective client delays in order to see which firms show the most interest. Wise proposal teams find ways to stay in contact with the DMU during this waiting period.

At the oral presentation, management will typically want to see the proposal team demonstrate insight into the business or industry. It wants to know that the firm will take the initiative in providing outstanding service and demonstrating responsiveness, and that the firm will work well with its organization.

It is also important to recognize that prospective clients usually want to address current and future issues, not past ones. Be cautious in addressing current problems; know the politics of the organization and the individuals of the DMU well before making any judgments. Do not risk antagonizing one of the decision makers by a misstatement. What is most important is that the proposal team demonstrate an understanding of the prospective client's plans and goals, both current and future, and focus on how the firm's services or personnel will help to achieve those goals. When making a proposal, proposal team members should remember that they are in the prospective client's house and should conduct themselves in the same courteous manner as at the site visits, even though the DMU members may now seem like old friends.

Parts of the Oral Presentation

Like a good business letter or report, an oral presentation has three basic parts: introduction, body, and closing. In addition, it provides an opportunity for questions and answers.

INTRODUCTION   The introduction comprises three elements:

1. A clear statement that the proposal team is there because your firm wants the business and believes it can do a great job
2. A brief rundown of the benefits to the prospective client that will be discussed more fully in the body of the presentation
3. An overview of what will happen following the appointment of the firm as auditors (this may be covered in the body instead)

BODY   Whether one person is organizing the oral presentation for the entire proposal team or the proposal team is planning it together, the first step in organizing the body of the oral proposal is to review the win strategy. If necessary, repeat the steps outlined in chapter 4:

1. Identify the members of the DMU (they may change roles).
2. Brainstorm to identify not more than seven key issues.
3. Put the key issues in order of importance to the primary decision maker.

The proposal team will then be sure to address first at the presentation those issues that are most important to the DMU members. In this way, the proposal team is more likely to gain and retain the prospective client's attention and convince it that the firm is truly concerned about its needs.

Benjamin Disraeli said, "Talk to a man about himself and he'll listen for hours." This holds true for the DMU as well. Talk to the DMU members about their concerns and priorities and the things that interest them, and they will listen to everything the proposal team has to say.

Remember that proposing is a process of persuasion. To succeed, the proposal team must demonstrate not only that it knows the issues, but also that the firm has the experience to deal with them. Each key issue or message in the body of the oral presentation should be organized persuasively, in the following way:

1. *Observation.* State the observation or recommendation that the proposal team wants to make.
2. *Benefit.* State the specific benefits of using your firm for the work identified in the observation or recommendation. (Remember to identify the benefits in terms of what the prospective client will be, do, gain, or save as a result of using the firm; see pages 33 to 34.)
3. *Feature.* Name the features or services the firm offers that will solve or address the problem.
4. *Proof.* Prove that the firm can do this with an example or endorsement, or with evidence (i.e., testimonials, facts, and figures).

For example, let's assume one of the points the proposal team wants to make is that your firm is experienced in making a smooth transition to a new auditor. One way to approach this could be in the following terms:

1. *Observation.* "You said you are concerned about what changing auditors will do to the already heavy work schedules of your financial staff."

2. *Benefit.* "You want to make the transition as easy as possible for your people. Our team has had the experience on nine occasions in the past three years of replacing other auditors. You will benefit from that experience because we can anticipate what needs to be done at every step of the way. We will come prepared and save valuable staff time needed for your hectic day-to-day schedule."

3. *Feature.* "One thing we can provide that will make the transition less disruptive for your staff is a computer-based worksheet with questions to be answered by your staff well in advance of our first visit. This information-gathering step can be scheduled into their routine work and entered into our audit software program before we visit the office for the first time."

4. *Proof.* "We used this approach when we took on the audits of ABC, XYZ, and BBR, and they found it to be very effective. Bob Johnson, the VP of finance at BBR, said that our approach to the transition was the most effective and the least disruptive of any he has experienced. We encourage you to contact Bob and some of our other references and discuss their transition experience with our firm."

Applying this approach to each of the key issues builds a compelling argument for selecting the firm.

CLOSING

In the closing, the proposal team has an opportunity to summarize key messages, review the features that distinguish the firm from the other proposing firms, and ask for the work. As in the proposal document, expressing eagerness to work with the prospective client is important.

QUESTIONS AND ANSWERS

A major reason for the question-and-answer session following the prepared remarks is to overcome objections, spoken and unspoken. At all stages of the proposal process, prospective clients are looking for reasons to eliminate contenders. It is important for the proposal team to confront these objections, as well as any other concerns, so that they won't eventually work against the firm. The proposal team cannot win the race if it does not seize the bull by the horns and deal with potentially damaging issues.

Tips for Preparing Qs & As in Advance

1. Throughout the proposal process, have a marketing professional or proposal team member keep notes on topics, hot issues, weak areas, and potentially hostile questions. These will vary significantly according to the circumstances of the opportunity and the volatility of the issues.

2. Develop and practice responses to tough or sensitive questions and to questions related to any key issues. (A list of possible questions is included in appendix E.)

3. Assign categories of questions to specific staff members to answer, including questions about any competitive weaknesses of the firm.

4. Agree on general procedures by answering these questions:
   - Will the lead partner catch all questions and pass them on to the appropriate proposal team member for an answer? (This is most desirable when central control is an issue.)
   - Will proposal team members jump in to answer? (This is usually not desirable unless it is planned in advance or the meeting is extremely informal.)
   - How will the leader be alerted to bail out a team member who inadvertently gets into trouble with his or her answer?
   - Will the leader restate a hostile question to refocus it or to emphasize the point the team wishes to make before answering? (This can be a useful technique when one person on the DMU strongly prefers another firm or is simply argumentative.)

Tips for Managing the Q & A Session

1. Repeat the question to be sure you heard it correctly.

2. Acknowledge each question without commenting on it or on the asker. For example, avoid saying "That's a good question" or "I'm glad you raised that." A silent pause is more effective and gives weight to your response.

3. Use eye contact, but address your answer to the whole group, not just the person who asked the question.

4. If the DMU members want to jump into the middle of the team's prepared remarks with questions, let them. If the proposal team has rehearsed both individual presentations and responses to possible questions, this will be no problem. In fact, it can demonstrate a high level of confidence, knowledge, and responsiveness.

5. Listen for the question behind the question and answer both. For example, if they ask how you will use technology to hold down fees, they may also be asking if the technology will disrupt their daily operations or if it will be available to their staff. Answer all these questions.

6. When answering a difficult question, use a technique called "shifting to the firm." For example, an auditor who is asked about his or her experience in multi-state taxation can answer that this is not his or her area. But instead of leaving it at that, the auditor volunteers information about the firm's expertise. Every proposal team member, whether a manager or a partner, is a representative of the firm, and as such is entitled to speak of the firm's collective expertise in any area.

7. Following the final question, repeat your big selling point and your call to action. You want the DMU to remember more than "Well, I guess that's it. Thank you."

The way the proposal team responds to the questions of the prospective client is an indication of how the team will serve the prospect as a client. If the proposal team members are open and friendly and not afraid to be sidetracked from the prepared text, they will seem much more confident and capable.

Organize the Oral Presentation

In the oral presentation, impact and style are everything. After all, the proposal team is selling specific people and their expertise, not a product that can be packaged in a box. To give the proposal team the best possible chance of winning, it is crucial to minimize the unknowns in the oral presentation. As early as possible after the presentation date is announced, the proposal team should meet to consider the audience, proposal team speakers, facilities and equipment, and visual aids.

AUDIENCE

If the firm has a contact inside the prospective client's organization, try to find out through this person the reaction of key decision makers to the proposal document and to those of the competition. Try to determine which firm, if any, holds the leading position going into the orals. It is appropriate to ask which members of the DMU might be advocates for competing firms. Those are the potential veto votes, and the proposal team needs to prepare a specific strategy aimed at neutralizing each one.

Proposal teams can be shortsighted in identifying the primary decision maker in the DMU. In some cases, especially in large companies, the DMU may change to a higher level of management from one meeting to the next. The new DMU may not have given the proposal document more than a brief glance and may be using the oral presentation to assess the people on the service team. Be prepared, for example, to learn on the day before the oral presentation that the CEO or chairman (whom the team members have never met) will attend the meeting and make the decision personally.

In planning the presentation, it is critical that the proposal team keep in mind the needs and point of view of the DMU members. Here are some questions to help the proposal team plan its approach:

- What type of presentation is the prospective client used to?
- Should the proposal team be formal or informal, laid-back or aggressive?
- To whom will the proposal team be speaking?
- Which member of the DMU will lead the meeting?
- Which service team member will lead the meeting?
- How will the proposal team react if there is an interruption or if the primary decision maker suddenly has to leave?
- How many of the prospective client's people will attend the meeting?

- How many of the firm's people should attend the meeting?
- Will new people be present whom the proposal team has not met? (Can we prepare for them?)
- Should the proposal team sit or stand?

THE ORAL PRESENTATION TEAM

The next step is to decide which members of the proposal team and which firm experts will attend the oral presentation. The following are some general guidelines for selecting speakers and planning their roles.

Who Attends?

Only those who will speak should attend the oral presentation. However, the proposal team may expand on this occasion to include an office managing partner, industry specialist, or firm chairperson, as appropriate. Normally, you should limit the oral presentation team to no more than the number of prospective client representatives present. A marketing representative may also be useful to help with presentation materials and to provide objective feedback after the meeting.

Who Is in Charge?

To demonstrate his or her leadership of the team, the team leader should usually be in charge. Everyone, including managing partners, should defer to the team leader during the oral presentation.

Where Will the Proposal Team Sit?

If the DMU members all sit along one side of the table, place the lead partner directly across from the key decision maker. Avoid sitting in presentation sequence. If random seating seems to be appropriate, the lead partner should try to face the key people. When in doubt, team members should sit across from the person to whom they need to deliver their selling message.

Who Says What?

The guiding rule in selecting speakers is that issues determine who speaks, not seniority. To determine speakers, make an informal worksheet that lists the key selling messages down the left side and the names of the DMU members across the top. Add any additional people who may be present, such as the CEO or CFO, a board member, or a representative from the parent company. Determine which issues are most important to which DMU members and put a check at the appropriate place on the chart. Exhibit 6.1 shows how the checklist might reflect this decision.

The most appropriate person to deliver each part of the presentation will be the member of the proposal team who has the most experience relevant to the particular selling point and who carries most weight with the target DMU members.

Be sure to identify the role of each speaker in such a way that the engagement partner is not overshadowed. Keep in mind that some prospective clients will want to meet the people who will be in their offices doing the work. Others will want a strong lead partner to manage the project personally and keep the

Exhibit 6.1   *Evaluating the Importance of Selling Points to the DMU*

Selling Points	Decision Makers				
	CFO	President	Chairman	Audit Committee	Internal Auditor
Transition experience (lead partner)	✔✔	✔			✔✔
New audit approach (senior manager)	✔✔			✔✔	✔✔
Competitive fees (lead partner)	✔✔	✔✔		✔	✔
Tax savings (tax partner)	✔✔	✔✔	✔		
Communication with audit committee (lead partner)	✔	✔	✔	✔✔	
Training for client's personnel (senior manager)	✔				✔✔
Merger & acquisition support (specialist)	✔✔	✔✔	✔✔		

Note: Two checkmarks denote greater significance.

staff in the background. Adapt your presentation to the preferred working style. A typical scenario involving the lead audit partner, the audit manager, the tax partner, and a specialist partner might unfold as follows.

1. *Introduction.* Senior partner opens the meeting, expresses enthusiasm and commitment, conveys one key sales message, and acknowledges the lead partner's ability. Lead partner then presents the major portion of the presentation.

    Note that very often the senior partner has no other role at the presentation than to convey how important the prospective client is to the firm. A senior partner, unless he or she is serving as an alternate or second partner, normally has little to contribute to the body of the presentation. However, it's best to have the senior partner provide the introduction. Don't underestimate the importance of this role. No one can enhance the credibility and convey the competence of a lead partner better than the senior partner who says, "I have known and worked with Jack for fifteen years, and I can assure you that he is one of the best partners in our firm. If anyone can do the job, he can."

2. *Body*. Key points are presented in order of importance to the DMU. The team member presenting each key point is the one who has the most actual experience with that subject and can provide examples from his or her own past work to prove it. One team member may present two or more points, depending on experience, not necessarily in sequence.

3. *Closing*. Lead partner summarizes the key selling messages and describes the distinctive features or services that will provide what the team has promised. Lead into questions and answers if these were deferred to the end of the presentation. Lead partner closes by repeating the primary selling message and asking for the work.

How Long to Speak?

A typical oral presentation is one hour, usually thirty minutes of prepared material and thirty minutes of Qs & As or discussion. No matter what the assigned timeframe, the proposal team will be wise to identify in advance expendable parts of the presentation. Each speaker needs to know what to drop from his or her presentation ahead of time, in case circumstances unexpectedly shorten the time available. Plan during the rehearsal what the expendable portions of each speaker's presentation will be or who will not speak at all, if necessary. The team must show no uncertainty during the orals.

FACILITIES AND EQUIPMENT

The following questions can help in deciding on facilities and equipment.

• Where will the presentation be?	An office is more informal than a boardroom.
• What facilities and equipment are available?	Find out what kinds of presentation are normal for the prospective client and tailor your firm's accordingly.
• May we visit the room beforehand?	Do so if possible to check seating arrangements, sight lines, and acoustics.
• Should we bring our own equipment?	In general, yes. You know how to work it and will not waste time fumbling.

VISUAL AIDS

Handouts and visual aids, such as slides and presentation boards, can greatly enhance the oral presentation. In most cases, the proposal team speaks to five or fewer executives, and poster-board-size signs or handouts are the most effective way to communicate the message. In general, it's wise to bring everything you need. Don't rely on the prospective client to have what you need in working condition.

Poster Boards

Poster boards are actually photostats increased in size by a camera at a typography house. The stats are on photographic paper that is then mounted onto a cardboard or foam-core back with adhesive. Depending on the complexity of the illustration, poster boards average about $100 to $150 each, including typesetting. Carrying cases (portfolios) are available from art supply stores to transport the boards to the meeting. Each holds about ten signs and costs about $100. You may wish to purchase a collapsible easel to hold the signs at the presentation.

Handouts

Handouts are often the most appropriate way to convey your message to a small audience. If used, they should stand alone—they need no explanation—and they should be distributed after the presentation. Handouts distributed during the presentation take the attention of the DMU away from your speakers. The DMU members will take notes on their own notepads; they do not need copies of your slides. If your presentation includes a complex process or graphic, make that one item a separate handout and use it only during your explanation. Handouts should convey your key selling messages and ask for the work.

Slides

Slides are appropriate for all sizes of audiences. In instances where the prospective client uses slides routinely for its own in-house communications, the proposal team may want to consider going to this added expense, especially since computer-generated slides are relatively inexpensive today. The price of slides (35mm) varies according to number of colors, the amount of text or graphic design involved, and the delivery time. Plan on an average cost of $25 to $40 per slide for three colors. An additional 200 percent rush charge per slide is common when a one-day turnaround is requested. Also, many office microcomputers have the capability to produce slides.

Overhead Transparencies

Overhead transparencies are appropriate for 10 to 20 people and are the most economical of all visual aids. They can be produced by a laser printer or a photocopy machine in your own office. They now come in colors, making the presentation more interesting visually. Stick to a pale blue or pale green background so that the text or illustration is readable. Do not use a dark background if you are planning to write on the transparencies. Take extra blanks in case you need to make a diagram.

Flip Charts

Flip charts are appropriate for small groups of three to five and can be prepared in advance and carried to the meeting. They should be professionally drawn and lettered by someone on the firm's staff or by an artist. While flip charts allow flexibility and spontaneity (they can be written on to emphasize points), they are awkward to carry and may crumple. Take a collapsible easel to ensure that the flip chart can be hung properly at the meeting.

Computer Slide Presentations

These are appropriate for groups of five or fewer (unless they can be projected onto a big screen). Many firms now use portable or desktop microcomputers to generate slide presentations. (Software costs range from $100 to $800.) The proposal team carries the computer to the prospective client's office and runs the presentation right on the computer. While this can be an effective and inexpensive way to make a colorful presentation, the potential weakness is that the presenters may not be familiar with the technology and run the risk of looking unprepared if something goes wrong. Be sure someone on the proposal team is adequately trained, just in case.

Video

Videos are appropriate for groups of 20 or fewer (unless they can be projected onto a big screen). Many larger firms use specially produced videos for significant proposal opportunities. This is an expensive undertaking—$20–$25,000 for a 6–10 minute film—and requires professional assistance. Since a quality video presentation can often look more polished than the team members actually presenting it or the other handout materials, use this method with caution so as not to diminish your effectiveness. Appropriate uses of video include animated graphics or statistics, taped interviews with key foreign team members, and taped testimonials from other clients regarding your firm's services. Recent technology breakthroughs include a desktop-computer slide format that incorporates live video footage on the screen with your computer-generated slides. It is a promising way to present a forceful presentation, but the equipment and software necessary to use it involve substantial costs.

Tips on Using Visual Aids

1. Visit the room in advance (take along the proposal advisor and make a sketch of the room elements).
   - Bring the firm's own equipment (or test the prospective client's).
   - Watch out for noisy fans (inside equipment or in the room) that impair hearing.
   - Note the shape of the table and number of chairs.
   - Ask where key DMU members usually sit.
2. When using poster boards, transparencies, or flip charts, remember that—
   - All charts should be either vertical or horizontal (preferred).
   - Two colors improve retention over black and white.
   - Initial caps and lowercase letters should be used on all text. An all-capital-letter format is harder to read.
   - List no more than seven items on one visual aid.
   - End with a summary chart of key points and display it until you leave the room.

3. Keep the lights on at all times, even when using slides.

4. Use a tabletop easel or flip chart for five people or fewer.

5. Use poster boards for nine people or fewer.

6. Overhead transparencies are okay for up to twenty-five people.

7. Offer the decision makers the best seats for viewing the visuals. The lead partner should face the decision maker and concentrate on his or her reactions to the presentation.

8. Use the format that is favored by the audience, not what is easiest for your team to produce.

9. The speaker stands with visuals to his or her left when facing the audience.

10. In developing visual aids, be sure that they will not dwarf or overpower the presenters. The proposal team should ensure that the focus of the decision makers is on the person speaking and not on the artwork or technology.

11. Have blank flip-chart paper, poster boards, or transparencies and suitable pens available when explaining complex questions.

Perfect the Oral Presentation

Rehearsing the presentation, using a critique team, and employing a coach can help the proposal team make a more successful presentation.

REHEARSALS

Rehearsing the oral presentation is critical to its success. The following are suggestions that can make the rehearsal process less painful and more productive. They can often make the difference between winning and losing the engagement.

To avoid problems created by schedule conflicts, plan rehearsals as far in advance as possible. As soon as the date for the oral proposal is known, the proposal team members should block out the two half days immediately preceding it on their calendars. The lead partner or office managing partner should arrange this meeting and mandate attendance by all team members who will be giving the presentation. Note that the lead partner's role in rehearsals is vital. His or her commitment instills commitment in the proposal team. Although it is possible for team members to work productively with members absent, the group dynamics that can make a presentation exceptional will be missing unless the commitment to practice is there.

Hold rehearsals in a place where there will be no interruptions. The ideal spot would be outside the office, but reality usually dictates a large conference room. Instruct all assistants and other personnel not to interrupt the rehearsals except in cases of real emergency. The rehearsal schedule allows time for the participants to go back to their offices and sign papers or return urgent calls.

Strongly encourage them not to get involved in any work that will take their concentration away from the rehearsal.

If the proposal team is not using a coach, it should plan to rehearse four times: once to establish the structure, once to videotape each presenter in order to delineate content and the use of visual aids, once to hear a critique team's comments and perfect the timing, and once to fine-tune the presentation and practice the answers to tough questions.

Tips for Rehearsing

1. Have a full-team discussion about who will present what material.
2. Run through each individual's part.
3. Videotape each individual (for private viewing) and at least one full-team rehearsal. This will pay the greatest dividend of all to your team, especially if you have no coach.
4. Be sure to hold at least one rehearsal at the exact time of day for which the oral proposal is scheduled. This will allow you to anticipate such subtleties as energy levels that drop after lunch, lighting, and distractions.
5. Have the full team meet for a minimum of two complete rehearsals of the presentation. If out of towners can't be there, send them a videotape of a rehearsal. Explain the overall strategy so they will arrive fully informed.
6. Time the last rehearsal or two. Remember that people will speak more slowly in front of the prospective client, so rehearsals should always run shorter than the time allotted.

CRITIQUE TEAM

A panel of partner reviewers can give the proposal team valuable feedback on the strategy and style of its oral presentation. The best reviewers are those senior managers or partners who—

- Have participated in two or more major proposals.
- Have special knowledge or experience in the industry or with similarly complex organizations.
- Don't mince words, but know how to critique without wounding egos.
- Are widely respected in the firm.

There are three ways to work with a critique team or review board. One is to give reviewers absolutely no background about the company or management's concerns, and then question them after the presentation to see if major messages were communicated effectively. Another way is to preview the proposal issues and the proposal team members' concerns, and then let the reviewers react to the oral presentation. The third way is to designate individual members of the critique team to assume the roles of key members of the prospective client's DMU. Provide the critique team with insights, biographical information, behavioral style, hot buttons, and anything else that may be relevant about particular DMU members. This method is especially useful for identifying questions that the prospective client may ask.

COACHES

An outside coach comes to the office a few days before the oral proposal, reviews the competitive situation, and reads the written proposal. At a full proposal team meeting, the coach reviews the key points to be made and helps identify the right people to make them.

Frequently, the coach wants to videotape an early run-through of the presentation to help team members evaluate themselves. He or she then works with individual team members to polish content and presentation delivery. The coach may also work with internal staff (or outside services) to develop any graphic support materials that the proposal team may use. The presentation may be videotaped again to check timing and observe improvements.

An oral proposal coach can be anyone who understands the proposal process, has the ability to help presenters change content or style, and is not afraid to voice what may be unpopular opinions. Usually, it is more effective to get a coach from outside your own office. Larger firms may have a number of trained people in the firm who can perform this role. For firms with more than one office, someone from another office will have instant credibility. Smaller firms do not have these resources, and must usually look outside the office.

An outside proposal coach should be chosen with care. Options include a public-speaking trainer from the company's public relations firm, a former marketing director from an accounting firm, a former TV anchor person, or a business development guru from an advertising agency. Any of these people can do a good job—but only if they know what is expected.

To get the most out of this strategy—

- Bring in the coach as soon as possible, long before the scheduled presentation. There can be no magic fixes at the last minute.

- Make sure the coach understands that he or she is expected to make a significant contribution to content, strategy, and organization, *not* to provide training in how to give a speech.

- Empower the coach to guide the process and give candid feedback.

- Brief the coach in advance about the overall strategy and competitive strengths and weaknesses of the firm.

- Brief the coach on the hot buttons of each DMU member.

Professional proposal coaches normally charge a daily rate. They expect to put in the same long hours as the proposal team and to attend or direct every meeting. The fee you can expect to pay varies according to location and the track record of the coach. In some cities, it may be as low as $500 to $750 per day. In New York, Chicago, Los Angeles, or San Francisco, expect to pay $1,500 to $2,000 per day.

Evaluate the coach on the effectiveness of his or her suggestions, not on the basis of whether your proposal won or lost. Investment in a proposal coach should be seen as an investment in a long-term relationship. The more a coach knows about the firm and certain of its personnel, the more effective he or she can be. If the coach is wise, tactful, and diligent, it won't take many proposal wins to recover the investment.

Chapter 7:
After the Oral Presentation

After the oral presentation, the proposal team may breathe a sigh of relief, but its work is not yet over. There are two tasks ahead. First, this is the time when winning proposal teams continue to develop their relationship with the prospective client. Second, once the prospective client reaches a decision, regardless of the outcome, the proposal team needs to assess what it did right and what it did wrong in order to benefit from the effort.

Follow-Up With Prospective Client

The designated spokesperson for the proposal team, usually the lead partner, continues to maintain contact with the prospective client. This can be done in a number of ways. The firm spokesperson can forward copies of relevant articles from the newspaper or trade journals, provide answers to questions raised during presentations, or provide assistance on a small project. The spokesperson could invite the tax director to attend, free of charge, an education seminar given by the firm or take the CFO or another member of the DMU to a cultural or entertainment event. The goal is to build on friendships begun during the proposal process and to demonstrate an ongoing concern for the prospective client.

Once the presentation is over, do not assume that you can sit back and wait for the decision. During the deliberation process, maintain regular contact with various members of the DMU. Be available to help solve problems or answer questions. Call to see how things are going. Your competitors will.

Conduct a Postmortem

Win or lose, proposing is expensive and time consuming. It makes good business sense to try and recover something for the resources invested in the process. Many firms use the period following the prospective client's announcement of the winning firm as an opportunity to learn from the experience.

IF THE PROPOSAL TEAM LOSES

Losing a proposal opportunity is always a disappointment, but a loss is not a failure. A loss simply means that the prospective client selected a proposal team that it perceived at the time met its needs more closely or that it knew better.

Proposal losses can be converted into future wins if the firm learns from its experience by conducting postmortem interviews with all prospective clients—those won as well as lost. This interview provides an impartial assessment of your firm's and your competitors' strengths and weaknesses. It eliminates the need to rely on speculation and enables the firm to profit from the experience in the future. Some firms follow up on proposal opportunities by calling or writing to the prospective client. Telephone calls are useful for maintaining contact after the proposal process, but a personal visit says to the prospective client that a lot of importance is attached to the interview.

Ideally, someone other than the lead partner who made the proposal—for example, the office managing partner—conducts the postmortem interview. It can also be helpful to take someone else along—the firm's marketing professional or partner, for example—for a different point of view.

The interviewer arrives prepared with a standard questionnaire or an outline of the information the firm wants to find out. Exhibit 7.1 provides a sample questionnaire. Upon returning to the firm, the interviewer drafts a summary based on the postmortem interview to distribute at the office. This summary can be used when an annual review is made of the firm's strengths and weaknesses in the proposal process.

Exhibit 7.1

Sample Postmortem Questions—Loss

1. What made you choose the winning firm?

2. Will the winning firm provide any special services or consulting work in addition to the audit [or other work you bid on]?

3. What were the most important criteria on which you based your decision?

4. What was the winning fee?

5. What should we do differently to improve our next proposal?

6. How much of a role did the written proposal play in the selection process?

7. What was the quality of our interaction with your management (frequency, communication style, etc.)?

8. What did the other firms do that you thought was especially good or helpful?

9. What can we learn from this experience that will help us to be better next time?

10. Would you consider hiring our firm to do special work or consulting projects in the future? Do you have anything in mind now?

The postmortem meeting can be an opportunity to let the prospective client know that the firm is still interested in performing other work for the prospective client. This leaves the door open for the lost client to consider the firm for other work in the future and gets your foot in the door again.

Postmortem meetings can also put the firm in the desirable position of service provider of second choice. Should anything cause the winning firm to withdraw, such as a conflict of interest or incompatible working styles, the provider of second choice stands to win the engagement without a second proposal.

IF THE PROPOSAL TEAM WINS

Postmortem evaluations provide an important opportunity even for the firm that has won an engagement. Returning to the new client with postmortem questions shows that the firm takes its work seriously and wants to do the best possible job. This impresses new clients. Exhibit 7.2 provides a sample questionnaire.

In addition, postmortem evaluations can provide useful and practical information for the future on major competitors. Today, many winning firms make a special effort to obtain copies of other firms' written proposals from their new clients. The information obtained can help the next time the firm proposes against those competitors.

Exhibit 7.2   *Sample Postmortem Questions—Win*

---

1. What made you choose our firm over the others?

2. What were the most important criteria on which you based your decision?

3. What was the most persuasive part of our proposal?

4. Were our fees competitive?

5. How much of a role did our written proposal play in the selection process?

6. Was our written proposal similar in style and content to the other proposals you received?

7. Did we have enough contact with your top management?

8. What did the other firms do that you thought was good or helpful?

9. What did we do that you thought was good or helpful?

10. What can we learn from this experience that will help us to be better the next time?

Appendix A:
Sample Requests for Proposals
(Questions to Be Addressed by Independent Accountant Candidates)

RFP Sample #1
(Detailed Format)

Background

1. Describe your firm's industry competence and specialization in the prospective client's (hereafter referred to as XYZ's) core entertainment businesses (supported by a representative listing of clients). Please indicate whether the work has been auditing and/or consulting and, if possible, describe the types of major engagements performed.

2. Identify partners of your firm who are recognized as specialists in our industry, including examples of their contributions.

3. Describe any positions taken by your firm with the SEC, AICPA, FASB, or FCC that could be viewed as controversial and that are relevant to our businesses.

4. What lawsuits are presently pending against your firm involving the SEC and, if relevant, what judgments have been made against your firm or its employees in the past three years?

5. Given that many of XYZ's core businesses are dynamic and complex, what commitments will your firm make to staff continuity? What has been your staff turnover in the Boston [or other appropriate offices] in recent years?

6. What investment banking firms and law firms has your firm dealt with in respect to our businesses? Which partners of these firms have you had continuing contact with, and may they be contacted?

7. Please comment on your experience and what views and/or resources you may have in helping your clients deal with various federal regulatory agencies (e.g., FCC, SEC, IRS, FTC).

8. Please identify the ten largest clients your firm (or office) has lost in the past three years and the reasons. Were any of these the clients of the partner who will be in charge of the XYZ account?

Technical Support

1. Define and discuss your firm's procedures for resolution of technical questions raised by clients or encountered during an engagement. Please be specific as to where the buck stops. When a decision is made by the engagement partner, is it binding on the firm or can it be reversed?

2. The internal audit function at XYZ is relatively new, having been in place for four years. Describe your firm's philosophy concerning working with and relying on internal auditing staff, and give examples of innovations in the way your firm uses internal auditors and the attendant cost reductions for external auditors.

3. Can you describe the strengths of your organization in providing investment advice (both tax and accounting) on the creation of joint-venture partnerships? (Many of our future transactions may be done on a joint venture basis with third parties.)

4. Do you have a position on technological obsolescence in industry and, relatedly, what are your recommended ranges for the useful life of our assets?

Engagement Team and Fee Proposal

1. Identify the partners and principal managers who would have substantial involvement in the engagement, and furnish biographical material on each.

2. Describe how your firm will approach the XYZ audit.

3. The international area is becoming increasingly important to XYZ. Please describe your international partners who would be assigned our account and your firm's international expertise in the entertainment industry.

4. The culture of XYZ is highly entrepreneurial, fast-paced, dynamic, and consensus-oriented in its decision making. Please describe how your firm can meet XYZ's demands for commitment, in depth knowledge of our core businesses, and, on occasion, immediate service responsiveness.

5. Set forth your fee proposal for the 19__ audit, with whatever guarantees can be given regarding increases in future years.

6. Furnish standard fee billing rates for classes of professional personnel for each of the last three years.

7. What has been your firm's [or *the Boston office's*] experience regarding realization rates of standard fees for audit engagements?

8. Although the technical and professional expertise of our independent accounting firm is important, we also believe that such a firm should exemplify a businessperson's approach to servicing our company. Please comment and/or demonstrate how this "street-smart" business aspect would be part of your firm's approach to client issues.

9. Please identify three to five clients of the partner who would be in charge of the XYZ audit and the names of the CFO and CEO to contact for references.

Other

1. Describe how important XYZ would be to your firm as a client.

2. Summarize how and why your firm is distinct from the other firms being considered and why the selection of your firm as independent accountants for XYZ is the best decision our company could make.

RFP Sample #2
(Short Format for Midsized to Large Companies)

The Audit Committee of our Board of Directors has asked us to evaluate our continued association with our current independent certified public accountants, as well as to consider other alternatives for obtaining audit and tax services.

I am therefore writing to ask for a proposal from your firm to provide these services to the XYZ Company.

If you are interested in conducting XYZ's annual audit and providing related tax services, please prepare a written proposal covering the topics outlined below, as well as any other topics you would like considered in our evaluation process.

XYZ Company Key Issues

1. What is the estimated time that XYZ personnel will require to teach your auditors about our businesses, systems, and procedures?

2. How will the audit fees reflect this learning curve (that is, how will the auditor's learning time be segregated from actual audit time, and who will absorb the cost of this learning period and any related travel or other expenses)?

3. What are your local office capabilities and availability, particularly regarding—
   a) Current client portfolio, industrial and construction materials available, and/or manufacturing experience?
   b) Strength in tax, EDP, consulting, and advisory services?
   c) Availability of engagement partners/managers throughout the year for discussion of technical audit, tax, reporting, and other issues?
   d) Staff rotation and assignment policies?

4. What are your other U.S. office capabilities and what is their proximity to XYZ's locations? What offices and services, particularly tax service capabilities, are available outside the U.S.?

5. What audit approach is used by the firm, particularly as it relates to—
   a) Utilization and reliance upon internal audit?
   b) Interim audit work and audit timing?
   c) Audit scope (EDP, pension plan, etc.) and materiality criteria?
   d) Use of remote office locations?

6. What will be the basis for the fee structure beyond 19__?

RFP Sample #3
(Informal Letter)

Dear [*Partner*],

I really enjoyed our meeting last week. The following day I met with Bob Johnson as you suggested, and he had some very insightful observations that have helped us quantify our expected results to the board. Thanks for the tip.

As I mentioned, we would like your firm to give us a proposal for our audit and other related services. We expect to accomplish a number of things in the next two years in which we could use your firm's help: an initial public offering, expansion of our domestic manufacturing capabilities, and installation of a new management information and reporting system. Please include your fee structure and how you handle related expenses and fee increases. If possible, we would like your proposal by next Wednesday, so that we can discuss it with you prior to our board meeting on Friday.

If you have any questions, please give me a call. We look forward to receiving the proposal.

Sincerely,

President
XYZ Company

Appendix B:
Sources for Prospective Client Research

Published (Print) Resources

Corporate Messages and Publications—If the prospect is a publicly traded company, review the past three annual reports especially well, paying careful attention to key words used by management that you can incorporate into your written and oral presentations. Also note variations in direction or emphasis in the chairperson's letter. If the prospect is a private company, some of the same information can often be obtained from the company's internal or client newsletters, marketing brochures, and other materials. Your purpose in scrutinizing these documents is to get a feel for the company's culture and the interests of its officers.

Standard & Poor's Register of Corporations—A directory of 45,000 public and private companies, subsidiaries, and affiliates. Each listing includes address, annual sales, SIC code, officers and directors, and accounting firm. By means of the index volume, companies in a particular industry or geographic location can be identified.

Moody's Manuals and *News Reports* (Industrial, Bank & Finance, Public Utility, Transportation, OTC Industrial, OTC Unlisted, International, Municipal & Government)—The basic manuals provide detailed corporate history, business developments, income and balance sheet data, plus officers, directors, and auditors for 22,000 companies and institutions. All information is taken from SEC filings. The *News Reports* are updated weekly and track major events such as mergers, joint ventures, executive changes, SEC filings, and so on.

Directory of Corporate Affiliations—A directory containing addresses, annual sales, officers, directors, and SIC codes for 4,000 parent companies and 40,000 divisions, subsidiaries, and affiliates. Excellent source for locating divisions of publicly held corporations. Companies are indexed by SIC code and geographic location.

Macmillan Directory of Leading Private Companies—Information on approximately 6,500 parent companies and wholly owned subsidiaries. Listings include address, SIC codes, officers and directors, sales range, and outside service firms, including auditors. SIC codes and geographic indexes are included.

On-line (Commercial Data Base) Resources

Dun's Market Identifiers—Contains records for almost two million U.S. business establishments (public and private) that have ten or more employees or one million plus sales. Contains address, SIC codes, business description, executives, number of employees, and more. Very useful for identifying companies in a specific geographic area, industry, or sales range. Auditors given for some companies. A highly manipulatable data base.

Standard & Poor's Daily News—General and financial information on over 12,000 publicly traded companies. Includes some Canadian and overseas companies. Includes annual report abstracts, interim earnings, management changes, mergers and acquisitions, bond ratings, litigation, SEC registrations, dividend announcements and changes, and statistical data. Print equivalent is Standard & Poor's Corporation Records Daily News and Cumulative News. Can be sorted and manipulated alphabetically and numerically with names, geographic names, SIC codes, sales data, and numerous other specific topics.

Standard & Poor's Register of Corporations—Identical to the print version, but information can be manipulated to create lists of companies meeting specific geographic, industry, sales, or auditor criteria.

Moody's Corporate Profiles—Contains abbreviated version of the information contained in the manuals. Included are 3,600 of the most important publicly held U.S. companies (all AMEX and NYSE, and 1,300 OTC). Information is easily sorted by address, SIC code, and various financial criteria.

Moody's Corporate News-U.S.—Current news on any of the companies covered in the five Moody's volumes—Bank & Finance, Industrial, OTC Industrial, Public Utility, and Transportation. Covers 13,000 publicly held companies. Information is sorted by SIC code, date, and topic (e.g., merger, executive change, joint venture).

PTS Prompt and PTS Prompt Daily—Excellent source for identifying companies, particularly smaller and private companies. Twenty trade journals are abstracted and added to the data base daily.

Disclosure and Compact Disclosure—Contains selected information from income statement, balance sheet, financial ratio, and business segment data, plus SIC codes, business description, officers, directors, and auditors for over 11,000 public companies. Information is extracted from various SEC filings and can be sorted in a variety of ways. Geographic location, SIC code/business description, auditor, sales, size, and other financial criteria are among the numerous sortable fields.

Laser Disclosure—Lists financial data exactly as presented in the 10-K or annual report. Searchable by company name, ticker symbol, and disclosure company symbol.

Lexis/Nexis—Includes over 100 newspapers: local papers such as the *Boston Globe*, business papers such as *Lehigh Valley Business*, industry papers such as

Advertising Age, and a few select foreign items such as *Current Digest of the Soviet Press*. The only U.S. on-line service with full text of *The New York Times*.

Business Dateline—Data base is excellent for identifying and tracking companies and individuals, especially smaller and private companies. Access to over 200 newspapers and magazines.

Dialong—An on-line system that contains the full text of approximately thirty-five local newspapers. More are being added at a rate of two or three a month. Good source for tracking local companies, executives, industries, and business trends.

Dow Jones News/Retrieval—The only full-text source for *The Wall Street Journal* and *Barron's*.

Newswires—Provide up-to-the minute full-text information on companies, executives, industry, and the economy. They are available on a number of on-line systems.

Firm Computerized Client Information—An in-house data base of client information. Locates firm clients by industry. Identifies partners/managers responsible for each client and their offices.

Dun's Marketing Service—This Dun and Bradstreet subsidiary will prepare customized mailing lists and labels from its data base. Company names can meet any number of customer-selected criteria (e.g., geographic location, sales size, and industry). The current charge is $78 per 1,000 companies (executive name and address with a minimum order of $450).

Sources of Information on Prospective Clients' Personnel

Published (Print) Resources

Most of the following sources contain the executive's corporate affiliations; only the *Who's Who* volumes and proxy statements contain more detailed biographical information.

- *Dun's Reference Book of Corporate Management*
- *Standard & Poor's Register of Executives*
- *Martindale-Hubbell Law Directory*
- Marquis' *Who's Who* directories
- Proxy statements

On-line (Commercial Data Base) Resources

- Standard & Poor's—Biographical (comparable to the print version)
- Marquis' *Who's Who* (comparable to the print version)
- Newspapers, business journals, trade/industry journals (available on numerous on-line systems)

Sources of Information on
Prospective Clients' Industries

**Published (Print)
Resources**

U.S. Industrial Outlook—Published annually by the U.S. Department of Commerce. Gives an overview of more than sixty-five industries and services including statistics, trends, and projections. Also lists sources for additional information.

Standard & Poor's Industry Surveys—Provides more detailed analysis than the Industrial Outlook, but for fewer industries. Trends, statistics, financial ratios for 1,200 public companies in twenty-two industries. An annual basic analysis is supplemented with quarterly current analyses.

Brokerage Reports—Investment firms issue industry as well as company reports. Use *Nelson's Directory of Wall Street Research* to locate analysts who track specific industries.

**On-line
(Commercial Data
Base) Resources**

Viewpoint and Investext—Full-text (except for graphics) of brokerage reports from selected investment bankers and brokerage firms. Industry and company reports are included.

Business Dateline—Full-text-articles from 140 regional business publications. Updated weekly, excellent for tracking industries, companies, business personalities in specific cities, metropolitan statistical areas (MSAs) or regions. Data base is searchable by geographic location, SIC code, date, person's name, company name, and topic (e.g., acquisitions and mergers, bankruptcy, going public, industry names).

Encyclopedia of Associations—An excellent source for identifying trade and industry associations that can be contacted for more detailed industry information.

PTS PROMPTS and PTS PROMPT DAILY—Comprehensive coverage of manufacturing and service industries. The data base consists of abstracts from trade and business journals, over two hundred local newspapers and regional business journals, news releases, newsletters, and industry studies. Information can be accessed using geographic codes, seven-digit product codes, event codes (e.g., mergers, new products, economic trends, market size/market share), company name, and date, among others. Excellent for tracking smaller and private companies.

Sources of Information on
Prospective Clients' Regions

U.S. Statistical Abstract, Dow Jones Irwin *Business and Investment Almanac*—Each source has an appendix that lists sources of state information. *The Statistical Abstract* lists state agencies and universities that publish state statistical abstracts. The *Dow Jones Almanac* lists state information offices and regional and state industrial and business directories.

Councils of Government—Councils of local governments, particularly economic development councils, can provide data and economic forecasts for regional areas within a state.

Chambers of Commerce—Most local chambers have publications on their cities and counties. Many can provide membership lists and directories of local businesses.

Metropolitan Insights (McGraw-Hill)—Contains key data and narrative analysis of 100 MSAs. Demographic profile, cost of living, construction data, and economic and business trends are covered for each area.

Local business journals and newspapers.

Sources of Information on Prospective Clients' Current Auditors

Published (Print) Resources

Who Audits America—Covers publicly traded companies only. The latest edition includes previous auditor and an IPO indicator for new public companies.

Standard & Poor's Register of Corporations—Has auditors for most of the 45,000 public and private companies, subsidiaries, and affiliates.

Moody's Manuals—All editions give auditor; information taken from SEC filings.

Corporate Finance Bluebook—Directory of the top 4,500 U.S. firms, including 1,800 private companies. Auditors are given for each company. The directory also lists the top officers and those with responsibility in financial areas. Contains a list of auditors and their clients.

Macmillan Directory of Leading Private Companies—The most comprehensive source for auditors of private companies. Contains a list of auditors and all their clients.

10-K Filings/Annual Reports—These, along with 8-K filings for auditor changes, are the most authoritative source.

Going Public—The IPO Reporter—Though complex and difficult to use, this source does give the auditors of companies planning to go public.

On-line (Commercial Data Base) Resources

Standard & Poor's Register of Corporations—The auditor field is searchable in this data base, making it easy to compile lists of accounting firms and their clients or a record of auditors in a particular industry.

Disclosure and Compact Disclosure—An authoritative source for auditor information. The data bases are searchable by accounting firm. Also tracks recent auditor changes.

Dun's Market Identifiers—This data base lists auditors for some of the two million records.

Appendix C:
Sample Proposal Documents

Chapter 5 discusses four kinds of written proposals. On the following pages are samples of each kind. To make it easier to compare them, all examples are from the health care industry. These proposals are real, but the potential clients to whom they were sent are not.

To facilitate comparison, the proposals have been edited to standardize the information presented. It is always tempting to create standardized text that describes your firm and some of the services it provides. Your goal in developing written proposals, however, should be to move away from standardized text and toward a proposal so specific that it cannot be used as the basis for any other proposal opportunity. It's a big challenge, and one you won't accomplish in a few months. The following text should therefore be used for informational purposes only, and not as the basis for your own boilerplate.

The prospective client's name and the names of all management personnel have been changed to ensure confidentiality. The fictitious accounting firm of Local & Local, CPAs, is the firm proposing to the prospective client, St. Charity Hospital, a major not-for-profit teaching hospital.

Example 1:
Statement of Qualifications

Mr. Thomas Thomson
St. Charity Hospital
123 Main Street
Ourtown, MA 98765

Dear Mr. Thomson:

Thank you for the opportunity to present our qualifications for the audit and concurrent management review of St. Charity Hospital for the year ending January 31, 19 __ . This letter describes the professional services that Local & Local, CPAs, can offer to meet your needs.

Health care is one of two major specialty areas for our firm, and we are well qualified to serve you. I have selected Sara Meyers, the co-director of our health care practice, to be your lead partner. If you have any questions about our qualifications or need more information, either she or I would be happy to answer them. We appreciate the opportunity you have presented to us and look forward to discussing our capabilities with you personally.

Sincerely,

Marion R. Clark, CPA
Managing Partner
Local & Local, CPAs

TABLE OF CONTENTS

I. THE FIRM OF LOCAL & LOCAL, CPAS

We very much appreciate the opportunity to submit our qualifications to serve St. Charity Hospital. This document aims at providing the Hospital with relevant background information about our firm and about some areas of our practice that we believe would be particularly relevant to you. As we move forward, we will attempt to develop a more focused understanding of the ways in which our range of capabilities can best be applied to meet St. Charity's needs.

Profile of Our Firm

Local & Local is based in Boston and we have offices in Worcester, Waltham, and Providence, Rhode Island. Our personnel comprises sixteen partners (including four health care specialists), thirty-three managers, and over one hundred staff accountants and consultants.

The firm was founded in 1963 and has grown steadily over the years. To strengthen our firm in the Northeast, we are also a member of the Continental Association of CPA Firms, Inc. This organization associates Local & Local with over one hundred independent firms in locations throughout the country, enabling us to offer a level of services comparable to that of most large accounting firms.

Commitment to Quality

The single most important factor in our firm's success over the past twenty-eight years has been our uncompromising commitment to the highest standards of quality and professionalism. Providing quality service to our clients is our primary objective, and we have developed review procedures and communications that ensure the highest standards of performance.

Local & Local has undergone its third peer review by the American Institute of Certified Public Accountants. This is a program dedicated to ensuring that participating firms have quality control systems in place over their accounting and auditing practices. This program also includes a review of our governmental client bases that have single audit requirements. We were pleased to receive an unqualified opinion and believe it reflects our commitment to quality work. We have also undergone a quality control review by the United States Department of Housing and Urban Development as mandated by the Single Audit Act of 1984. The audit selected for review was accepted without change.

II. SPECIALIZED HEALTH CARE INDUSTRY PRACTICE

St. Charity Hospital should take note of the strategic commitment to health care organizations on the part of our firm's senior management. Health care is one of only two industries our firm's Management Committee has selected for major long-term investment. That means we dedicate top-quality talent and substantial resources to ensure that we stay abreast of emerging industry issues so that we can serve our clients better. Our investment in the health care industry practice has led to an average annual growth rate of 15 percent per year for the past three years.

Our Health Care Specialty Group is charged with keeping our clients and our own professionals informed about significant developments in the industry, and about the impact of these developments on the management and operations of health care providers. It accomplishes this through participation in industry associations and activities, publications, special programs, and other means. Our industry group responds to the needs of our health care clients as management consulting professionals. The group consists of four partners and twenty professionals with specialties and expertise gained, in many cases, through prior experience in the health care industry. Their backgrounds include experience in—

- Registered records administration.
- Data processing and systems consulting.
- Hospital administration.
- Nursing.
- Materials and office operations management.

Members of this group stay abreast of the latest in health care developments, policies, and issues nationwide.

Industry Activities

Members of our Health Care Specialty Group are actively involved in a wide spectrum of industry activities. They participate frequently as speakers at technical meetings and as authors of articles for professional publications.

Strength of Our Health Care Practice

We serve as independent accountants for many large hospitals and health care organizations. Our clients are in both the provider and payer sectors and include clinics, medical groups, and managed care and public-sector practices.

Some of our hospital and health care clients include the following:

- Barnes Hospital
- Children's Hospital of Boston

- HealthEast
- Jewish Hospitals of Boston
- Leominster Hospital
- St. Luke's Hospital (Worcester)
- Sudbury Critical Care
- University of New Hampshire Medical School
- VHA/Massachusetts
- Yankee Alliance

Services we can provide to our clients cover all areas of interest and concern to health care providers, including—

- Hospital auditing.
- Tax compliance and planning.
- Third-party reimbursement, including appeals.
- Cost accounting.
- Revenue enhancement.
- Nursing.
- Clinical program definitions.
- Operations improvement.
- Business office operations, including accounts receivable and medical records management.
- Strategic and financial planning.
- Management information systems.

III. AUDIT AND OTHER SPECIALIZED SERVICES

While the range of services provided by most accounting firms has expanded significantly, audits continue to be the dominant aspect of our practice. We reject the idea that an audit is a commodity. In the course of carrying out an audit, your accounting firm should generate information and develop insights that will result in improved controls and safeguards leading ultimately to greater efficiencies and clear, concise, and understandable financial reporting that is respected by the financial community. Our professionals combine competence with judgment, maturity, and creativity—all prerequisites for a quality audit.

Highest-Quality Audit Services

Our audit will be made in accordance with generally accepted auditing standards and will include tests of our accounting records and other procedures we consider necessary to expressing an unqualified opinion on the financial statements.

If, for any reason, we are unable to render an unqualified opinion, we will discuss the reasons with you and the alternative report that could be issued.

Our goal will be to perform our work with as little interruption to your daily work as possible. All individuals involved in the audit will be certified public accountants with health care experience. One important aspect of our management review will be interviews of key office personnel and the physicians. We will schedule these at your convenience and, whenever possible, written questionnaires will be used.

We will present the financial statements, our audit report, and our letter of recommendations to the Audit Committee and Board of Directors and answer any questions that the Directors might have.

Audit Approach

Our audit approach is based upon a risk-oriented perspective and entails—

- Deepening our understanding of your business policies, procedures, markets, and objectives.

- Evaluating systems, processes, and people that control and process transactions or monitor and evaluate risk.

- Testing the ability of your systems to process and report transactions accurately.

- Reporting the results of our testing clearly and usefully to management and the Board of Directors.

We will make every effort to use schedules and analyses already prepared for internal purposes and eliminate unnecessary duplication of effort between our staff and yours.

Tax Services for Health Care Clients

Local & Local provides tax planning and compliance services to hospitals and related entities in a wide range of areas, including the following:

- Reorganization and structure
- Tax structuring of joint venture arrangements
- Unrelated business income tax matters
- Information reporting requirements
- Employee benefits
- Information reporting requirements
- Fund-raising activities
- Arbitrage restrictions and disclosure requirements

Our health care tax specialists analyze tax-exempt health entities, their business activities, and the types of transactions they re-engaged in, to assess potential tax implications and provide tax-related recommendations. These specialists can assist St. Charity Hospital with a full spectrum of tax services, as needed.

Consulting Capabilities for Health Care Clients

Building on the experience gained from our existing client base, we continue to invest professional and financial resources in delivering a wide range of services to the health care industry. We understand the needs of the health care industry because we serve so many facets of it—through a multifacility system, long-term and residential care, managed-care facilities, major teaching hospitals, and alternative delivery systems. We also work with clients developing new health care concepts, such as PPOs, HMOs, indigent care programs, super nursing stations, product-line management, and regional health care systems.

We offer a comprehensive array of consulting services that compares favorably with some of the largest firms in the country.

Our services are especially strong in—

- Third-party reimbursement.
- Cost containment and productivity.
- Business office operations.
- Operations improvement and revenue enhancement.
- Data processing.
- Managed care/alternative delivery systems.
- Strategic, financial, and facility planning.

We would be pleased to provide references or further information on any of our services at your request.

Example 2:
Fee Proposal

Board of Directors
St. Charity Hospital
123 Main Street
Ourtown, MA 98765

Dear Board Members:

On behalf of Local & Local, CPAs, I am most pleased to present our proposal to serve as independent accountants for St. Charity Hospital.

St. Charity is the most prestigious organization of its kind in Massachusetts and one of the leading providers of health care services in the Northeast. We will commit our top resources to meet your specialized service needs.

The following are among the key points of our qualifications:

- A health care practice that numbers more than fifty health care clients, including many distinguished hospitals, clinics, and health care providers

- A commitment to assign to St. Charity our top-rated health care audit partner and senior audit manager—Sara Meyers and Bob Brown—to serve you

- A clear position of leadership in Massachusetts among providers of accounting, auditing, and tax consulting services

- A full range of service capabilities, including a recognized specialization in health care and health care tax issues, together with numerous related management consulting services

Health care is one of only two industries that the senior partners of Local & Local have designated to receive a top-level, firm-wide commitment of resources and support. The opportunity to gain St. Charity as a client is of great importance to us. Our firm is committed to building on our existing health care and not-for-profit practice, as well as developing a hospital practice in Massachusetts. Within this context, St. Charity would be our largest client.

During the transition period to our firm, Sara Meyers, Bob Brown, and the other key Ourtown personnel assigned to serve St. Charity will have no other significant client responsibilities. In addition, Tom Burns, another of our firm's highly experienced health care partners, will spend at least four weeks on-site in Ourtown during our first year's service. Tom and Sara will head the strategic planning meeting described in Section 2 of our proposal and will work closely with the hospital's management and our service team on an ongoing basis to help ensure the effectiveness of our services.

As managing partner of our firm, I will also personally see to it that the hospital has prompt and ready access to our best people, both locally and firm wide. We will spare no effort to understand and meet your expectations. Again, I thank you for this opportunity to present our proposal. We look forward with great enthusiasm to serving you.

Sincerely,

Marion R. Clark, CPA
Managing Partner
Local & Local, CPAs

TABLE OF CONTENTS

I. CREDENTIALS AND QUALIFICATIONS

According to national surveys, the health care industry will be structured very differently in the year 2000. Local & Local wants to be able to help clients to prepare for and meet the challenges they will face in the years ahead.

Strategic Focus on Health Care

St. Charity Hospital should take note of the strategic commitment to health care organizations on the part of our firm's senior management. Health care is one of only two industries our firm's Management Committee has selected for major long-term investment. As a practical matter, that investment in the industry translates into the dedication of our top-quality talent, sustained attention and effort, and substantial resources to achieve certain key objectives:

- Meeting our own criteria, including outstanding personal service marked by leadership, technical expertise, and responsiveness
- Staying abreast of—and ahead of—emerging industry issues, so that we can assist our clients in understanding and responding to them

Our investment in the health care industry practice has led to an average annual growth rate of 15 percent per year for the past three years.

Health Care Specialty Group

Our Health Care Specialty Group is charged with keeping our clients and our own professionals informed about significant developments in the industry. We help to assess the impact of these developments on the management and operations of health care providers through participation in industry associations and activities, publications, special programs, and other means. Our industry program responds to the needs of our health care clients and includes a network of accounting and auditing, tax, management, and consulting professionals. The group consists of four partners and twenty professionals with specialties and expertise gained, in many cases, through prior experience in the health care industry. Their backgrounds include experience in—

- Registered records administration.
- Data processing and systems consulting.
- Hospital administration.
- Nursing.
- Materials and office operations management.

Members of this group stay abreast of the latest in health care developments, policies, and issues nationwide.

Industry Activities

Members of our Health Care Specialty Group are actively involved in a wide spectrum of industry activities. They participate frequently as speakers at technical meetings and as authors of articles for professional publications.

Strength of Our Health Care Practices

We serve as independent accountants for many large hospitals and health care organizations. Our clients are in both the provider and payer sectors and include clinics, medical groups, managed care, and public-sector practices.

Representative Clients

Our hospital and health care clients include the following:

- Barnes Hospital
- Children's Hospital of Boston
- HealthEast
- Jewish Hospitals of Boston
- Leominster Hospital
- St. Luke's Hospital (Worcester)
- Sudbury Critical Care
- University of New Hampshire Medical School
- VHA/Massachusetts
- Yankee Alliance

Services we can provide to our clients cover all areas of interest and concern to health care providers, including—

- Hospital auditing.
- Tax compliance and planning.
- Third-party reimbursement, including appeals.
- Cost accounting.
- Revenue enhancement.

- Nursing.
- Clinical program definitions.
- Operations improvement.
- Business office operations, including accounts receivable, management, and medical records.
- Strategic and financial planning.
- Management information systems.

II. OUR SERVICE TEAM

We have selected our premier service team to work for St. Charity Hospital. The members of this group cumulatively possess more than thirty years of experience serving hospital systems and other health care organizations.

Qualifications and Roles of the Service Team Members

Sara Meyers will be the engagement partner. She is a senior partner in our firm, and has more than twenty years of experience. Sara has an extensive background in directing auditing and accounting services for hospitals and other health care clients. She is one of our firm's top specialists in health care, and is the co-director of our Health Care Industry Specialty Group. In addition to her experience in directing audits, she has experience in the important area of reimbursements. Sara's clients have included Children's Hospital of Boston, HealthEast, Jewish Hospitals of Boston, Leominster Hospital, and Shared Medical Technologies.

Bob Brown will serve as audit senior manager. He has more than twelve years of experience, including two years as associate director of Saint Anthony's Hospital in Phoenix. Bob is a health care specialist for our firm and has hands-on experience with all the aspects of hospital management. His clients have included Children's Hospital of Boston, Leominster Hospital, Richland Memorial Hospital, St. Luke's Hospital (Worcester), and Mercy Medical Clinic.

Tom Burns will act as a special advisory partner for St. Charity. He brings more than twenty years of experience serving health care industry clients, and serves as co-director of our Health Care Industry Specialty Group. Tom has provided acquisition-related audit and due-diligence services to investment bankers on health care industry transactions. He has also directed feasibility studies for financings through tax-exempt bonds, and has participated in operations and productivity studies and business office reviews. Tom's clients have included Barnes Hospital, Johns Hopkins Medical Center, Stanford University Medical Center, Children's Hospital of Boston, Jewish Hospitals of Philadelphia, NorMass Medical Center, St. Vincent's Hospital (New York), Presbyterian Hospital, and Medical Associates Clinic.

Sara and Tom will draw on other experienced staff and health care specialists in our firm as needed to ensure an audit and business advice of the highest professional caliber.

Strategic Planning Meeting

We propose to conduct a strategic planning meeting at our expense to initiate our services for St. Charity Hospital. Such a meeting would serve a number of important purposes:

1. Identify key concerns and priorities of the hospital's management in an efficient and economical way so that those priorities can be built into our service approach from the beginning

2. Stimulate innovative thinking and fresh insights into immediate and longer-term decisions the hospital must make in terms of operations, finances, and other concerns

3. Assist in developing constructive working relationships and positive inter-actions between the hospital's management and our team

4. Ensure the full involvement of our firm's top resources from the very outset

III. OTHER CAPABILITIES

Tax considerations are increasingly important for health care organizations in today's environment. Cutbacks in public funds have led not-for-profit entities to move into for-profit ventures. This, in turn, raises concerns about preservation of tax-exempt status, minimization of unrelated business income tax, and ultimately, examination of the corporate structure in response to these issues.

The IRS is scrutinizing closely the activities of tax-exempt organizations for issues regarding unrelated business income and inurement of benefits. Congress is studying methods of increasing tax revenues of not-for-profit entities.

Tax Services for Health Care Clients

Local & Local provides tax planning and compliance services to hospitals and related entities in a wide range of areas, including the following:

- Reorganization and structure
- Tax structuring of joint venture arrangements
- Unrelated business income tax matters
- Information reporting requirements
- Employee benefits
- Fund-raising activities
- Arbitrage restrictions and disclosure requirements

Our health care tax specialists analyze tax-exempt health care entities, their business activities, and the types of transactions they are engaged in to assess potential tax implications and provide tax-related recommendations. These specialists can assist St. Charity Hospital with a full spectrum of tax services, as needed.

Consulting Capabilities for Health Care Clients

Building on the experience gained from our existing client base, we continue to invest professional and financial resources in delivering a wide range of services to the health care industry. We understand the needs of the health care industry because we serve so many facets of it—through a multifacility system, long-term and residential care, managed-care facilities, major teaching hospitals, and alternative delivery systems. We also work with clients developing new health care concepts, such as PPOs, HMOs, indigent care programs, super nursing stations, product-line management, and regional health care systems.

We offer a comprehensive array of consulting services that compares favorably with some of the largest firms in the country. Our services are especially strong in—

- Third-party reimbursement.
- Cost containment and productivity.
- Business office operations.
- Operations improvement and revenue enhancement.
- Data processing.
- Managed care/alternative delivery systems.
- Strategic, financial, and facility planning.

Sara Meyers will draw on the resources of our firm that can help St. Charity achieve its immediate and longer-term goals.

IV. PROFILE OF OUR FIRM

Local & Local has the strength of its personnel and its diverse and prestigious clientele. We are a major provider of services to health care organizations in New England. (See Appendix B for a partial listing of our clientele.) None of these, however, is comparable in size or stature to St. Charity Hospital. The hospital will be assured of receiving the level of attention and resources due a flagship client.

Our firm has four offices: our headquarters in Boston and offices in Worcester, Waltham, and Providence, Rhode Island. Our personnel comprises sixteen partners (including four health care specialists), thirty-three managers, and over one hundred staff accountants and consultants.

The firm was founded in 1963 and has grown steadily over the years. To strengthen our firm in the Northeast, we are also a member of the Continental Association of CPA Firms, Inc. This organization associates Local & Local with over one hundred independent firms in locations throughout the country, enabling us to offer a level of services comparable to that of most large accounting firms.

Commitment to Quality

The single most important factor in our firm's success over the past twenty-eight years has been our uncompromising commitment to the highest standards of quality and professionalism. Providing quality service to our clients is our primary objective, and we have developed review procedures and communications that ensure the highest standards of performance. We will continue to rely on our proven policies and control procedures to anticipate St. Charity's needs and avert any problems.

Quality Control

Local & Local has undergone its third peer review by the American Institute of Certified Public Accountants. This is a program dedicated to ensuring that participating firms have quality control systems in place over their accounting and auditing practices. This program also includes a review of our governmental client bases that have single audit requirements. We were pleased to receive an unqualified opinion, and believe it reflects our commitment to perform quality work. We have also undergone a quality control review by the United States Department of Housing and Urban Development mandated by the Single Audit Act of 1984. The audit selected for review was accepted without change.

V. PROFESSIONAL FEES

Our fees are based on the time spent on the engagement and the billing rates of the individuals assigned. Although we have strong credentials in the health care industry, our firm is nevertheless smaller than the other firms you have asked to propose, and our overhead rates are lower. We pass those savings along to clients like St. Charity. This can be an important factor in your decision. Our goal is to help you contain your costs. With Local & Local, you get industry prominence at a reasonable rate. Based on our experience in other similar engagements, our proposed fees are as follows:

Examination of the statement of assets, liabilities, and equity of St. Charity Hospital as of January 31, 1993 and the related statements of income and expenses and retained earnings for the year then ended, and report to the Audit Committee and Board of Directors	$34,000
Management review of the systems and procedures of St. Charity Hospital, issuance of report, and recommendations	$11,500

The estimated fees exclude out-of-pocket expenses, which will be billed separately. Our fees for tax and consulting services, as in other areas of our practice, are based on the time actually spent on a given project at hourly rates that reflect the experience levels of the professionals involved. Our policy is always to reach an agreement with client management about our projected fees before beginning work.

We do not bill for responses to client questions that require no significant investment of research time or other costs. Providing a high level of value for the fees you pay is integral to our basic engagement philosophy.

In all cases, we will thoroughly discuss the scope of the services to be provided with the appropriate members of St. Charity's management and achieve a mutually agreeable decision as to estimated time, fees, and services to be rendered.

Fees for subsequent years will be adjusted to reflect the level of inflation in the Consumer Price Index. Given the size and importance of St. Charity's operations, we believe that our professional fees represent a fair value.

Although fees are important, they should not, in our view, be the determining factor in the selection of an accounting firm for St. Charity Hospital. The choice of independent accountants and business advisors should always be made primarily on the basis of qualifications, capabilities, and commitment.

We will spare no effort—now or in subsequent years—to find common ground for providing the level of services St. Charity requires, at a reasonable cost.

APPENDIX A: RESUMES OF OUR SERVICE TEAM

[Insert resumes for each member of the service team through the supervisory senior level and for any industry specialists or other named consultants who may serve the prospect.]

APPENDIX B: REPRESENTATIVE CLIENTELE

[Insert appropriate list of firm's clientele.]

APPENDIX C: REFERENCES

Like most professional services firms, we could make endless claims about our expertise and record of service. Performance is what counts—and performance is something for which only our clients can really vouch. We urge you to contact our clients to see for yourself what kind of work we do and the kind of service our professionals provide. Following are a number of clients who are very familiar with our firm and, particularly, with the qualifications of our proposed service members.

[Insert names, addresses, titles, and phone numbers of two references for each of the key members of the service team.]

Example 3:
Reproposal or Retention Proposal

Mr. Thomas Thomson
St. Charity Hospital
123 Main Street
Ourtown, MA 98765

Dear Tom:

Over the years, we have enjoyed working with you and we welcome this opportunity to remind you of our qualifications to serve St. Charity Hospital. Industry challenges and competitive pressures have increased substantially in recent years, and we look forward to continuing the teamwork we have shared as you pursue your business objectives. You know our track record of providing the Hospital with effective and efficient audit, tax, and consulting services. And you know our service team and our working style. The relationships we have all worked to build are a strong foundation on which to move forward together.

An update of our qualifications and credentials is presented for your convenience in the following pages. We are confident that our resources and the service strengths we bring to St. Charity will demonstrate that the firm you know best is also the most highly qualified to serve the Hospital today and in the future. As you and the board know from our efforts during the recent Senate investigation, we deliver what we promise—the highest quality and professionalism.

Yours truly,

Marion R. Clark, CPA
Managing Partner
Local & Local, CPAs

TABLE OF CONTENTS

I. THE PAST YIELDS TO THE FUTURE

For more than ten years, Local & Local has been part of the St. Charity family of service providers. We have been privileged to share in the excitement of the changes and accomplishments you have experienced. This shared tradition is not something that happens over weeks or even months. To develop the necessary level of understanding takes years, and St. Charity's management will, no doubt, consider this carefully in its review process. As you explore your options, we want you to remember several points that we believe make us the right choice for St. Charity in the future, as we have proved to be in the past.

St. Charity has been on the forefront of not-for-profit hospitals in the nation, struggling with funding issues, unprecedented growth, and other challenges that major teaching hospitals have faced in the 1980s and 1990s. Local & Local has been there with your hospital every step of the way, and we look forward to serving you as you create your future.

Local & Local is proud to provide your auditors and tax consultants. St. Charity is an outstanding organization; we have both benefited from our long association. We want to continue to serve you. Of the many attributes that make us eminently qualified, four stand out:

1. The dedication and experience of our people—people who know your business and, more importantly, your hospital

2. Our exceptional capability in areas of special interest to St. Charity

3. The depth and breadth of our expertise in the health care industry

4. A commitment we share to provide superior client service and the highest technical quality

Exceptional, Experienced Professionals

More important to St. Charity than our list of clients is the caliber of the people we have assigned to serve you—we have selected some of our best. Sara Meyers, engagement partner, and Bill Durry, tax partner, have each served St. Charity for ten years. Bob Brown and Marie Kennedy have each served St. Charity for at least five years. They provide a continuity of understanding no other firm can hope to match. You have had many opportunities to observe their responsiveness and commitment to the Hospital, especially since the changeover of your records system. With Local & Local, you will have no wasted time training new accountants.

As the engagement partner, Sara Meyers orchestrates the services and support you require from us. She is one of the most respected senior partners in our firm. As a member of our firm's Management Committee and co-director of our Health Care Industry Specialty Group, she is responsible for major decisions that affect all of our clients. As you have observed throughout the years, Sara ensures that our resources are coordinated efficiently to provide added value and support to St. Charity in achieving its business objectives.

A History of Distinguished Service to St. Charity

Because Local & Local has served St. Charity during its ten years of most dramatic change, we have a clear understanding of the qualities you require from your public accountants—qualities such as responsiveness, creativity, technical excellence, and outstanding relevant industry and functional expertise. Because our team of professionals has demonstrated these qualities, we have been able to help you through some of your more difficult transitions. For example, last February, when the Senate subcommittee on medical ethics and education investigated the charges of news organizations that new physicians are inadequately prepared for the complexities of modern medical practice, Sara and staff spent more than 150 hours supporting your senior management as they prepared their testimony. The length of our relationship has been a benefit to us in delivering responsive, effective service.

Local & Local is a proven resource in supporting and assisting St. Charity in the accomplishment of its goals. As you move forward beyond the transitional issues, you will face many other challenges and choices. Your hospital will benefit immediately, as it has in the past, from our breadth of knowledge and understanding of how large hospitals are managed and governed. Our firm has been there to provide support, solutions, and expertise during your most crucial period of change. Our knowledge and experience will continue to help minimize the disruptions that significant change can bring.

II. AUDIT EFFICIENCY THROUGH CONTINUITY

Sara Meyers and the other individuals who manage our audits of St. Charity have considerable experience with the Hospital and the industry. You have come to know the members of our audit team and their working styles well.

As mentioned before, Sara is responsible for ensuring that our audits are conducted effectively, efficiently, timely, and in a manner beneficial to St. Charity. She will continue to ensure that all the resources and appropriate specialists of our firm are introduced to the Hospital as required. As the lead partner, she is the primary contact for St. Charity's management and will continue to ensure that all issues are appropriately resolved, and that we are responsive to all of the Hospital's needs.

Continuity is extremely important in performing an effective audit of St. Charity Hospital. Our rotation policy, as demonstrated in the past, is to assign management to the Hospital for the maximum period allowable under AICPA rules. Since the Hospital is a private organization, your lead partner may continue in that role for as long as the Hospital wishes. Other professionals will be rotated periodically to help them develop their expertise and professional skills. Such rotations, as you have observed in the past, will be conducted in an orderly way, designed to minimize the impact on St. Charity's audit. We will continue to consult with you about changes at appropriate times.

Highest-Quality Audit Services

While the range of services provided by most accounting firms has expanded significantly, audits continue to be the dominant aspect of our practice. We reject the notion that an audit is a commodity. In the course of carrying out an audit, your accounting firm should generate information and develop insights that—in the hands of professionals who combine competence with judgment, maturity, and creativity—will result in improved controls and safeguards leading ultimately to greater efficiencies and clear, concise, and understandable financial reporting that is respected by the financial community. Our track record with St. Charity speaks for itself.

Leadership in Your Industry

Among all but the largest consulting organizations in the country, Local & Local's auditing, tax, and consulting services to the health care industry are unsurpassed, as demonstrated throughout this document. Not only do we audit fifty hospitals and health care organizations, we also provide leadership to the industry within our own profession. As an example, one of our partners recently participated in writing the new AICPA 19__ Audit and Accounting Guide *Providers of Health Care Services*. Others have leadership roles in professional organizations, such as the Hospital Financial Managers Association and the Health Care Management Special Interest Group of the American Medical Association.

A Service Philosophy Based on Value

First and foremost, we are in business to serve our clients, to help them solve their problems and achieve their business objectives, and to make a solid contribution to their success and profitability. From our newest recruit to the top management of our firm, our people work to identify and respond to our clients' needs. We devote significant resources to ensuring that we meet our high standards. We share St. Charity's commitment to delivering services of exceptional quality.

III. SPECIALIZED SERVICES

Local & Local has unsurpassed specialty capabilities that will be important to St. Charity Hospital as it charts its future course. As a result of our commitment of resources and extraordinary skill in supporting our health care clients, we have accumulated an immense amount of experience and developed innovative approaches. For example, when the Hospital was threatened with a malpractice suit two years ago, our health care specialists worked together with Hospital management and our litigation support specialist to develop materials prominent in the Hospital's defense. As your attorneys told us at that time, we were instrumental in your acquittal and in the subsequent appeal.

Although we do not have the resources of the largest firms, our consultants have extensive capabilities in the areas most important to St. Charity. As you continue to build your infrastructure, modify your management information and records systems, and develop innovative arrangements with physicians, our professionals will draw on their expertise to ensure the best possible service in keeping with your needs.

Over the years, St. Charity has been served by several of our industry specialists, including Tom Burns, co-director of our Health Care Industry Specialty Group. Tom's efforts were key in the successful installation of your new patient billing system, which, to quote your director, Karla Samson, "is the best in the industry." We will continue to provide specialized services as special concerns or needs arise.

Strategic Tax Services

Our tax professionals understand that your tax services and overall tax strategy must be driven by your business strategy—not developed in a vacuum. You and your independent tax advisors must coordinate the myriad tax laws and integrate them with the strategic goals of the Hospital.

We have already gained a significant appreciation of your major concerns based on our past and current working relationship. Our tax service team is prepared to address these concerns and assist in ethically maximizing St. Charity's current and long-range cash flow by minimizing tax payments. Because we know your business, your industry, your management teams, and your structure, we bring additional value and the assurance of the most efficient use of St. Charity management's time in the development and implementation of tax strategies.

Bill Durry will continue to provide his expertise in not-for-profit taxation. He is highly regarded by his clients for his client service skills and in-depth understanding of tax matters unique to not-for-profit hospitals. He assists a number of our largest clients in tax accounting methods and compliance matters, including assistance with administrative proceedings and examinations by taxing authorities. He will continue to ensure that St. Charity's tax needs are met, as he has for the past ten years.

APPENDIX A: ABOUT OUR FIRM

Local & Local's strength is the quality of its personnel and its diverse and prestigious clientele. We are a major provider of services to health care organizations in New England. None of these, however, is comparable in size or stature to St. Charity Hospital. As our flagship health care client, you receive the highest level of attention and resources due one of our most important clients. You will continue to receive responsive, attentive service.

Our firm has four offices: our headquarters in Boston and offices in Worcester, Waltham, and Providence, Rhode Island. Our personnel comprises sixteen partners (including four health care specialists), thirty-three managers, and over one hundred staff accountants and consultants.

The firm was founded in 1963 and has grown steadily over the years by adding new services that our clients need. To strengthen our firm in the Northeast, we are also a member of the Continental Association of CPA Firms, Inc. This organization associates Local & Local with over one hundred independent firms in locations throughout the country, enabling us to offer a level of services comparable to that of the largest accounting firms.

APPENDIX B: OUR SERVICE APPROACH

Our firm's business strategy is to focus on our strengths and provide outstanding client service. We define our strategy by the needs of our clients, not by the actions of our competitors.

Commitment to Quality

The single most important factor in our firm's success over the past twenty-eight years has been our uncompromising commitment to the highest standards of quality and professionalism. Providing quality service to our clients is our primary objective, and we have developed review procedures and communications that ensure the highest standards of performance. We will continue to rely on our proven policies and control procedures to anticipate St. Charity's needs and avert any problems.

Each business we audit is unique. Therefore, individual audits require planning that is tailored to particular operations and financial reporting requirements. Our audit approach is based on a thorough understanding of the business. No other firm has the understanding of St. Charity Hospital that we have. Our personnel place a high priority on maintaining effective working relationships with the hospital's personnel. Those relationships take years to build, and result in a higher standard of audit than you could expect for several years from another firm.

Quality Control

Local & Local has undergone its third peer review by the American Institute of Certified Public Accountants. This is a program dedicated to ensuring that participating firms have quality control systems in place over their accounting and auditing practices. This program also includes a review of our governmental client bases that have single audit requirements. We were pleased to receive an unqualified opinion, and believe it reflects our commitment to perform quality work. We have also undergone a quality control review by the United States Department of Housing and Urban Development as mandated by the Single Audit Act of 1984. The audit selected for review was accepted without change.

Clear Communication

As you have experienced over the years, we at Local & Local value the candid exchange of ideas and opinions with our clients, and we appreciate that the hospital shares this view. We strive to maintain an open door with management. Our key team members will continue to meet with hospital management frequently and be available whenever you wish to meet with us. We want to continue to respond to your needs.

Clear communication includes providing cost-effective recommendations for improvements. To conclude our audit, we perform a subsequent events review, obtain management representations, issue our report on the financial statements, and issue a management commentary letter. As we did in the last quarter, we will place particular emphasis on providing meaningful business advice in connection with the audit.

Our team members are always alert to opportunities for improvements in operational and reporting efficiency. We are proud of the work that we perform and of the thought that goes into our management commentary letters.

APPENDIX C: RESUMES OF OUR SERVICE TEAM

[Insert resumes for each member of the service team through the supervisory senior level and for any industry specialists or other named consultants who may serve the prospect.]

Example 4:
Letter Proposal

Mr. Thomas Thomson
St. Charity Hospital
123 Main Street
Ourtown, MA 98765

Dear Mr. Thomson:

Thank you for the opportunity to meet with you, Susan, Paul and Frances. We are pleased to present our qualifications for the audit and concurrent management review of St. Charity Hospital for the year ending January 31, 19 __ . This letter describes the professional services that Local & Local, CPAs, can offer to meet your needs.

Local & Local was organized in 1963 and continues to experience substantial growth. We have grown into a reputable regional firm, especially in the health care industry. We offer St. Charity the best of two worlds—the experience and expertise of a regional firm, combined with the attention and focus of a dedicated local firm. We are truly large enough to meet your needs, yet small enough to deliver the responsive service you expect. Health care is one of two major industry focuses for us.

There are three significant reasons why we believe we are distinct from other firms that want to serve St. Charity:

1. We are a leader in New England in providing audit, tax, and business advice to the health care industry.

2. We offer a broad-based management consulting practice composed of highly experienced health care management professionals to supplement our audit. They are ready to assist St. Charity Hospital in virtually any management, operations, or financial area.

3. The service team we have selected—from supervisory senior to partner—has more than thirty years of combined experience serving major hospitals and other health care clients.

Representative Clients

Some of our hospital and health care clients include the following:

- Barnes Hospital
- Children's Hospital of Boston
- HealthEast
- Jewish Hospitals of Boston
- Leominster Hospital
- St. Luke's Hospital (Worcester)

- Sudbury Critical Care
- University of New Hampshire Medical School
- VHA/Massachusetts
- Yankee Alliance

Our Service Team

Sara Meyers, audit partner, assisted by Bob Brown, audit senior manager, will be responsible for all services provided to St. Charity. Sara is one of the most respected senior partners in our firm, and serves as a member of our firm's Management Committee and co-director of our Health Care Industry Specialty Group. Sara would ensure that our resources are coordinated efficiently to provide value and support to St. Charity in achieving its business objectives. Her clients have included Children's Hospital of Boston, HealthEast, Jewish Hospitals of Boston, Leominster Hospital, and Shared Medical Technologies.

Bob Brown has more than twelve years of experience, including two years as associate director of Saint Anthony's Hospital in Phoenix. Bob is a health care specialist for our firm, and has hands-on experience with all issues of hospital management. His clients have included Children's Hospital of Boston, Leominster Hospital, Richland Memorial Hospital, St. Luke's Hospital (Worcester), and Mercy Medical Clinic.

In addition, Sara will from time to time draw on the special expertise of Tom Burns. Tom has more than twenty years of experience serving health care industry clients, and serves as co-director of our Health Care Industry Specialty Group. Tom has provided acquisition-related services on health care industry transactions and has directed feasibility studies for financing and participated in operations and productivity studies and business office reviews. Tom's clients have included Barnes Hospital, Johns Hopkins Medical Center, Children's Hospital of Boston, Jewish Hospitals of Philadelphia, NorMass Medical Center, St. Vincent's Hospital, Presbyterian Hospital, and Medical Associates Clinic.

Tax and Management Consulting Services

We have found from experience that audit services are only a fraction of the services required by a not-for-profit hospital. For some of our clients, we function as the primary management and fiscal advisor to the executive director, board of directors, and controllers. We are available at all times to offer advice on any fiscal and management matter in which you need assistance.

Our tax department consists of seven partners and thirty professionals. A number of these have extensive health care and/or not-for-profit experience. They are knowledgeable in all aspects of the tax questions and filings required by both the federal government and the state of Massachusetts. As part of our engagement, we would prepare federal and state of Massachusetts information returns and other registration reports as required for that year.

Our computer department and management consulting professionals can provide advice in various information systems-related areas, including patient billing, third-party reimbursements, and management information. We are familiar with the system you are currently installing, and will be able to interact efficiently and intelligently with it.

Audit Scope and Objectives

We would audit the balance sheet of St. Charity Hospital as of January 31, 19__ and the related statements of activity and cash flows for the years then ended. Our audit will be conducted in accordance with generally accepted auditing standards. The financial statements are solely the representation and responsibility of the hospital's management. Our responsibility is to express an opinion on them based on our audits.

If we become aware of any errors, irregularities, illegal acts, or certain matters involving deficiencies in the internal control structure and its operation that we consider to be reportable conditions under the standards established by the AICPA, we will communicate them to you. At the conclusion of each year's audit, we will submit to the hospital's Board of Directors a report containing our opinion on the financial statements. If, for any reason, we are unable to render an unqualified opinion on the financial statements, we will discuss this with you and the hospital's management in advance.

Audit Administration

We anticipate that in late fall of 19__ we will hold a planning meeting that will include representatives of your Board and management. This meeting will be at our expense and is part of our investment in a long-term relationship. At our meeting, we will discuss and schedule our preliminary audit fieldwork and discuss your expectations. After completion of the year-end fieldwork, we will hold an exit conference with you to discuss management letter points and any other audit issues. Finally, we will present the audit report and management letter to the Board of Directors. This will give the Board an opportunity to discuss any questions or concerns regarding the hospital and its operations. Our experience has shown that this enables the Board to better understand the fiscal operations of the hospital.

Estimated Fees

Our fees are based on the time spent on the engagement and the standard hourly billing rates of the individuals assigned. Our fees for this engagement are based on the following hourly rates:

Partner	$100–$125
Health care specialist partner	$150–$250
Manager	$60–$90
In-charge	$40–$55
Staff Assistant	$30–$40

Although we have strong credentials in the health care industry, our firm is smaller than the other firms you have asked to propose, and our overhead rates are lower. We pass those savings along to clients like St. Charity. This can be an important factor in your decision. Our goal is to help you contain your costs. With Local & Local, you get industry prominence at a reasonable rate. Based on our experience in other similar engagements, our proposed fees are as follows:

Examination of the statement of assets, liabilities and equity of St. Charity Hospital as of January 31, 1993 and the related statements of income and expenses and retained earnings for the year then ended, and report to the Audit Committee and Board of Directors	$34,000
Management review of the systems and procedures of St. Charity Hospital, issuance of report, and recommendations	$11,500

The estimated fees exclude out-of-pocket expenses, which will be billed separately. Fees for tax and consulting services, as in other areas of our practice, are based on the time actually spent on a given project, at hourly rates reflecting the experience of the professionals involved. Invoices will be rendered monthly and are due and payable in thirty days. A 2 percent discount is available for invoices paid by the 25th of the month following billing. We reserve the right to suspend services if the balance due in your account includes invoices that are 120 days or more in arrears. We will provide you with a full accounting of time and billing charges on an interim basis at your request.

These fees are based on the understanding that the overall condition of St. Charity Hospital's financial and accounting records is excellent and that we will receive the support from the hospital's personnel necessary for the preparation of requested schedules and other supporting documentation as previously indicated in this proposal. If conditions are such that our audit procedures result in a reduction in this fee, you will be charged the lower amount and not the fee estimated in this proposal.

Summary

We believe the foregoing meets the requirements of your Request for Proposal, but if you have any questions, please let us know. We would be pleased to discuss this proposal with you at any time. Thank you again for the opportunity to propose. We believe that as you review the qualifications of all the firms you will find Local & Local well qualified to provide you with the services you require. We look forward to working with you and the personnel at St. Charity Hospital.

Very truly yours,

Marion R. Clark, CPA
Managing Partner
Local & Local, CPAs

[Additional pages of detailed resumes may follow this page.]

Appendix D:
Sample Fee Presentations

Example 1

Professional Fees

Our fees are usually based upon service time on an engagement at hourly rates related to the experience levels of the individuals assigned. We believe that the following key features of our plan for serving ABC Company will enable us to control our fees, both now and in the future, while maintaining the highest standard of quality.

Coordination and Advanced Techniques

We will coordinate our efforts with Mr. _____ and his staff to avoid duplication of work and increase efficiency. We will use the most advanced auditing techniques available to the profession to ensure that we perform exactly the required amount of testing and concentrate our audit work on areas of greatest potential risk.

A Fresh Look

We will conduct a review of ABC's operations and related internal accounting controls to gain in-depth knowledge of your organization. The purpose of this review is twofold. First, it will provide us with the knowledge of your operations that we need to conduct an efficient, quality audit. Second, and equally important, it will provide you with the opportunity to take a fresh look at your procedures, systems, controls, and reports to assure yourselves that your financial and management information systems are in sync with your overall business needs.

The review will be conducted by the engagement team we have selected to serve you. It will be joined, as required, by various firm industry and functional specialists. We expect the review to involve approximately _____ hours, including _____ partner hours. The cost of such a review represents an investment on our part that ensures you will receive responsive service on an ongoing basis. This is part of our operating philosophy to provide added value to our clients.

Rate Structure and Fees

Our rate structure is comparable to that of other CPA firms of our size. We believe that our approach, however, is more efficient than that of other firms. We have observed this to be true when we have succeeded other firms as auditors. It is our efficient approach that allows us to maintain a high quality of services at a reasonable cost.

Our fees in future years will not increase from those quoted, unless there are significant changes in the scope of your operations or in the scope of the work we are asked to perform. We will adjust our fee periodically in response to the effect of inflation on our salaries and related costs.

Our policy is not to surprise you. We will review our fee estimates with your management each year before beginning our audits. We would expect to discuss with you, in detail, requests for any additional professional services and to provide you with an estimate of our fees before commencing any additional work.

Estimated Fees

Based on our discussions, we anticipate that our first year's fees will be $_____. Any out-of-pocket expenses will be billed separately. We are committed to providing comparable levels of service in succeeding years at the same rate, subject only to inflation or changes in the scope of services required.

The transition from your current firm will involve a substantial investment on our side. We will absorb all of the costs involved in that transition so that ABC management can budget the cost of our services accurately. Making this investment is one way we demonstrate to you our interest in establishing a long-term relationship.

[*If you plan to provide any free services, such as a management consulting review, tax planning, or executive financial services, insert a paragraph to describe those services here. Include the usual cost of those services so that the prospective client understands their value.*]

Estimated Hours

Our estimated hours for the specified audit services you have discussed with us are as follows:

	Year Ended December 31	
	199__	*199__*
Financial statement audit		
Partner		
Manager		
Staff		
Compliance audit		
Partner		
Manager		
Staff		
Hourly Billing Rates		

Our billing rates for professional staff vary, depending on the experience of the individual and his or her seniority. The following are the ranges for our professionals' time:

Partner (industry specialist)	$150–$250
Partner	$100–$150
Senior Manager	$90–$120
Manager	$60–$100
Senior	$50–$70
Staff	$30–$60

As we mentioned in our discussions, we are very excited about the opportunity to serve ABC company. If you have any questions concerning our fees or the scope of our work, please let us know.

[*You may prefer not to provide the hourly billing rates or the actual hours you anticipate providing unless specifically asked to do so. If you consider that you will gain a competitive advantage from doing so (for example, against a major firm whose rates may be higher), then be sure to provide a range of rates in order to give yourself flexibility in billing the work later.*]

Example 2

Professional Fees

The professional fees presented in this section are based on our best assessment of the time and resources required to provide audit and tax services for the various ABC entities for the year ending December 31, 19 __ . Our rates depend on the level of expertise required to deliver the required services, the time of year the services must be delivered, and the amount of recurring services.

We believe that professional fees should be evaluated according to the quality and value of the services delivered. During the proposal discussions we studied your business, including your plans and strategies for the future. You anticipate continued growth. The professional assistance you receive in preparing for and managing this growth can have a significant impact on your operating results. We are confident that we can add significant value to your business during this important phase of ABC's development.

We are also mindful of your need to conserve resources and control costs. As professional advisors, we will share management's cost concerns, working closely with ABC personnel to enhance the efficiency and cost-effectiveness of our services. Our first-year costs normally exceed the costs of recurring work. With this in mind, and with the prospect of developing a long-term and mutually beneficial relationship with ABC, we will absorb all costs of transition and all start-up costs associated with our work for ABC. These costs are our investment in a relationship that we expect to be mutually beneficial and satisfying for many years.

We will spare no effort—now or in subsequent years—to find common ground for providing the level of services ABC requires. And at a reasonable cost. We want client relationships in which we can make a fair profit on our services while delivering value that exceeds our fees. We will never ask you to pay a fee that you do not believe to be fully justified.

Out-of-Pocket Expenses

In addition to the fees quoted below, we will bill you for any out-of-pocket expenses incurred in delivering services, such as travel expenses and computer tax return processing charges.

Recurring Audit Services

Following is our proposed level of fees and hours, as you requested. We have also provided a detailed breakdown by subsidiary. Although the complexity and volume of transactions will vary among the various entities, we have spread the cost evenly at your request. The actual billing per entity can be provided in future years, should you desire such a break out of fees.

[*Insert a table or chart here that shows each entity and the estimated fee.*]

Recurring Tax Services

Our fee estimates assume that—

- Your in-house computer system will generate tax-basis property records and will calculate tax-basis depreciation.

- If feasible within the constraints of your in-house computer system, you will code your general-ledger accounts with tax sorting codes and provide us with computer-readable trial balances.

- Partnership agreements (if any) and other critical documents will be available for our review prior to November so that we can review them and agree with you on the tax construction of these agreements prior to December 1.

[Insert a table here that lists entities or individuals and the estimated fee for U.S. and individual state tax returns.]

These fee estimates are indicative of the fees we would charge in future years, assuming that the scope of work does not vary significantly in subsequent years.

Nonrecurring Tax and Accounting Services

As we previously indicated, we are convinced that there are opportunities for us to add enormous value to your business as you experience growth. Our fees for tax and accounting consulting services will be based on the experience and skills of the individuals who are needed to provide the services. In these specialized areas, the value you receive from our services will frequently exceed our actual fees by a wide margin.

Example 3

Professional Fees

We expect our professional accounting and auditing fees to total $_____ for 19 __ . This amount includes the statutory audit and related filings, as well as periodic meetings with ABC's management and Audit Committee. It does not include out-of-pocket expenses, which we will bill separately. The fee for other services, such as tax or management consulting, will be billed as 80 percent of our normal billing rates on an hourly basis. As you require these special services, we will meet with you to discuss the scope of the work and provide you with an estimate at that time.

Our philosophy is a simple one—you will have no surprises on fees. We will discuss our work with you in advance and provide you with a written estimate. Unless the scope of the work changes, that is the bill you will receive. We are excited about the opportunity to work with ABC's management, and do not want fees to be an impediment to your selection of our firm.

Appendix E:
Sample Questions From
Oral Presentations
(May Be Used to Rehearse Answers in Advance)

Audit Management

Why can't you run our engagement without partners in the field?

How do you determine which facilities will receive full-scope/limited-scope operational audits?

What are the steps you will take to ensure a smooth transition?

How will you work with our Audit Committee?

You just won the audit for ABC, a direct competitor. If you become our auditors, how will this affect the confidentiality of our information?

What steps have you taken to provide us with services uniquely suited to our needs, not duplicated from those of ABC?

We appreciate the attention we have received from your senior managers. What ongoing relationship do they actually have with a new client like us?

Explain how the technical review process works within your firm.

How do you propose to handle communication with our management?

We want no surprises at year-end. How will you ensure that?

Since we are not one of the largest clients of your office, how can we be sure of your attention and responsiveness?

What does "businessman's approach" mean in regard to the audit?

How will you ensure uniformity of the worldwide audit?

How will you obtain a basic understanding of our operations and activities in planning the audit?

To what extent and how would reliance be placed on internal auditors as members of the team?

How is the quality of an audit engagement controlled? Is any special review of SEC filings required by an SEC specialist and, if so, where is this specialist located and does he/she have expertise in our industries?

How do you expect to know if things get out of control, and will you tell us?

What exactly did you do to make those transitions effective for your other clients?

The approach you suggest is completely different from what we are doing now. Why are you so certain that it is the right approach?

Cost

How did you arrive at your fee estimate?

Your fee is much lower than our current fee. Are you performing less work for us? Will you be available when we need you?

How do you plan to hold down your fee?

Could our fees be further reduced if we provided additional hours of internal audit assistance?

Some of the other firms we have met with offer a lower fee. Are you willing to negotiate on your proposed fee or give us a fee guarantee for three years?

How will you control fees overseas?

How much of your actual out-of-pocket expenses will we be billed?

We were hoping to get a lower fee. Where could we cut corners to save a little more and still use your firm?

What role do you see our Internal Department playing in the audit on a year-round basis? What adjustments could you make if we were unable to provide you with the level of support planned, and how much would our fee increase?

Do you ever decrease your fees?

Industry Expertise

Describe your practice in our industry in this city.

What do you believe will have an impact on our industry and our company over the next five years? Why?

In our audit, what areas would you consider high risk and what areas low risk?

What is the future of leasing as a tax-deferred method for our industry?

What do you think of our business?

What are the most critical areas of risk in our business? How can we limit our exposure?

**Additional
Services**

We operate in twenty-six states. How can you help us reduce our state and local tax exposure?

What assistance can you provide in structuring joint ventures, restructuring debt, reimbursement problems, Capitol Hill contacts?

How can your firm help us identify potential merger partners or acquisitions?

In what ways could you help us identify possible acquisition candidates? How would you charge us for support in these efforts?

Can you introduce us to your other clients and arrange business deals for us?

Some of these tax ideas look interesting. Will our effective rate go down immediately if we use them?

No one has addressed the issue of our recent divestitures. How do you think we are progressing, and do you see any problems?

If we were to retain our current auditors, would you be willing to perform tax work for us?

Timing

How much time will the lead partner (or industry specialist) spend on our engagement?

How many hours have been budgeted for the industry expert's time?

What proportion of your time and the audit manager's time will actually be spent at our facilities?

How much time can our staff expect to spend on transition activities over the next six months?

How long will it take for you to review our systems and write your programs?

We expect to make a number of changes in the financial area in the next few months and think that perhaps we would like to postpone changing auditors for one year. Are you willing to wait?

Staff

Explain the difference between the roles of Mr. Smith (lead partner) and Mr. Jones (managing or client service partner).

Do you have enough staff people familiar with our industry to handle both our and the ABC (a major competitor) engagements?

Who is the head of your national group in our industry? Where is he or she located?

Describe how you plan to staff the job below the manager level and how many people there are at what locations and during what time periods.

Can you provide some examples of the financial and tax planning strength of your personnel?

What is your policy on staff and partner rotation?

Confidentially, we are not sure that the manager you have proposed to us will work well in our environment. Can you change your team?

Who will be the actual final authority on our audit?

Who will actually control the subsidiary audits? How will they be staffed?

In our experience, firms often send in their top experts to sell us consulting services and then remove them, leaving worker bees of lower quality. Are you committed to having the people referred to in this proposal actually do the work?

The lead partner's bio shows a number of large clients who are not his/her clients now. How can we be certain that you'll stay with us for the seven-year period you say you will?

Do the people on this team represent the best retail experience you have available locally?

Can you provide the staff to ease our busy periods?

With two partners seemingly in charge of our account, which one will we see the most of? Who will actually be in charge?

Have the members of this team worked together before?

You have indicated in your proposal that the lead partner will spend a lot of time in our offices. Our experience is that when there's lots of partner time, the costs of the accounting services invariably go up. Do we need all of this attention?

How difficult will it be for your people to learn our methods?

We have experienced a lot of auditor staff turnover from year to year. Can you guarantee continuity (or that we will not be a training ground for inexperienced staff)?

How do you ensure recruitment of the best college graduates?

Firm Reputation   Your quality image has been linked with a conservative approach. Can you explain?

Why has your practice in our city shrunk?

Have you lost any major clients lately? Why?

Do you have any significant lawsuits pending? What is your litigation record?

Firms are collapsing and merging today. How can we be sure that yours is financially sound and will be around next year?

How did you select your references?

I seem to remember reading that we had a problem with your firm on an audit of our Brazilian operations some years ago. Do you know what that was about?

Ethics

Was your firm one of the firms sued by the FSLIC in the savings and loan failures? Discuss your litigation record.

What would be your reaction if we asked you to approve a position outside of GAAP/GAAS?

How would you handle a conflict of interest if you were approached by our major competitor?

How would you identify fraud in our organization? Who would you report it to?

Working Style

What is your firm's policy about referring its clients to other clients for business deals, such as joint ventures? What about purchasing the products of your clients?

What is the availability of software packages for use by your staff and our internal auditors? How would our internal auditors be trained to use such software? What fees would be charged?

Would your firm provide us with details of budgeted and actual hours to perform the audit?

What would you do if we asked a question and you didn't know the answer?

Will you give us straight talk whenever you see potential problems—even if your team caused the problem?

How will you work with our new CFO when he comes on board?

We want to comply with the various reporting requirements of our parent company, but we basically operate independently and like it that way. How can you convince me that you will not communicate all our business activities back to the parent company, serving as its eyes and ears in monitoring us?

You have shown us your willingness to respond quickly to our various requests over the last few months. How can we be sure that this level of service would continue once we are your client?

Miscellaneous

Do you have any questions for us?

What do you believe are the most important criteria we should consider in selecting a CPA firm?

We have had our current auditors for nearly twenty years. Why should we choose you over them?

Who is your client—the audit committee or management?

We want to retain our current firm for corporate and personal tax work. If your firm performs the audit, how will you coordinate with that firm?

What is the one thing you would bring to us that no other firm could bring?

Your proposal document makes some pretty strong statements about ways our current firm has failed to meet the mark. On what do you base those claims? Can you give examples?

As a director on the board of several other publicly traded corporations, I have had occasion to review audit proposals from several firms. Despite differences in presentation and promises, all the firms seem to say more or less the same thing. Why should we pick you when we already know our current firm and are happy with the level of service it delivers?

Appendix F:
Services and Publications
of the Management of an
Accounting
Practice Committee

CONFERENCES

Call (212) 596–6139 for additional information on conferences.

National Practice Management Conferences, targeted at the managing partners of local firms, offer a practical approach to practice management. They are geared to mid-size and larger local firms, but open to all. Two conferences annually: summer and fall.

National Small Firm Conferences, designed for sole practitioners and firms with two or four partners, provide practical guidance on operating a successful small firm. As with all MAP conferences, exchange of information on management problems and solutions with other practitioners is emphasized. Two conferences annually: summer and fall.

National Marketing Conferences are designed primarily for partners responsible for marketing and marketing directors of firms of all sizes. The conferences cover techniques for successful practice development. One annual conference.

SERVICES

Local Firm Consultation Program offers an intensive review of your firm's administrative procedures and advice on management practices. The two-day consultation, conducted by two experienced CPA practitioners with firm management responsibility, produces constructive suggestions, solutions to specific problems, and a fresh view of your practice. Call (212) 596–6136.

The MAP Inquiry Service responds to member inquiries concerning firm management and administration. If you need more help, the MAP staff will put you in touch with experienced CPAs or consultants who can assist you with special problems. Call (212) 596–6139.

PUBLICATIONS

Except where listed, call AICPA Order Department at (800) TO–AICPA (800–862–4272) or 201–938–3000 (outside U.S.).

MAP Handbook, a comprehensive 1,000-page, three-volume loose-leaf reference service on practice management, is updated annually. It includes more than 200 forms, sample letters, checklists, and worksheets, all easy to reproduce or adapt for your practice needs. It provides detailed financial data and policy information, for firms of various sizes, that enable you to compare your performance with that of comparable firms. Topics covered include developing an accounting practice, administration, personnel, partnerships, and management data. For information call (212) 596–6137; to order call (800) 323–8724.

MAP Selected Readings, a companion book to the MAP Handbook, is a readers' digest of over 500 pages of articles on successful practice management, specially compiled from leading professional journals. The articles contain numerous profit-making ideas for your practice. A new edition is published annually. For information call (212) 596–6137; to order call (800) 323–8724.

MAPWORKS–DOCUMAP contains on diskette documents from the *MAP Handbook* dealing with organization, client engagements, and personnel. Available in three formats: APG2—No. 016911, ASCII—No. 090080, and WordPerfect 4.2—No. 090081.

On Your Own! How to Start Your Own CPA Firm provides nuts-and-bolts advice on how to start a CPA firm. It contains a wealth of hands-on information on operating profitably of use to new and established firms, as well as to prospective firm owners. Product No. 012641.

Organizational Documents: A Guide for Partnerships and Professional Corporations is a guide to drafting a partnership agreement and corporate documents. The book includes a sample partnership agreement with more than 100 provisions and a step-by-step approach to incorporating. Book: No. 012640; WordPerfect 4.2 disk: No. 090091; ASCII disk: No. 090090; Book and WordPerfect 4.2 disk set: No. 090096; Book and ASCII disk set: No. 090095.

Management Series booklets cover the issues your clients are dealing with now. Designed to help you help your clients solve their management problems, the series includes *Management of Working Capital* (No. 090060), *Financing Your Business* (No. 090061), *Making the Most of Marketing* (No. 090063), *Managing Business Risk* (No. 090062), and *International Business* (No. 090064).

Practice Continuation Agreements: A Practice Survival Kit explains how you can preserve the value of your practice in the event of death or disability. A practice continuation agreement can prevent the value of your practice from dissipating, provide financial and emotional benefits to your family, and help fulfill your professional responsibility to your clients. Product No. 090210.

Managing the Malpractice Maze offers firms specific techniques for lowering their risk of liability. It identifies criteria for evaluating a firm's existing defensive practices program and shows how to develop such a system if one is not in place. The book also features a ten-step plan to follow when a claim is brought and discusses such vital management issues as practicing without insurance, documenting engagements, selecting an attorney, and implementing a quality control system. Product No. 090380.

Managing By The Numbers: Monitoring Your Firm's Profitability assists you in your efforts to improve your firm's long-term financial performance. It helps you identify immediate opportunitites within your firm and provides you with a dynamic tool to manage your practice better on a regular basis. This book instructs you step-by-step how to examine the numbers behind the numbers and uncover situations that may not be obvious in conventional financial statements. Product No. 090220.

The *MAP Roundtable Discussion Manual* contains guidelines for organizing a MAP roundtable discussion group. Such a group can help firms find practical solutions to common problems through regular meetings and information exchange. The guidelines include sample correspondence, forms for administering a roundtable, and nearly forty suggested discussion outlines on topical management issues. To order call (212) 596–6139.

UPCOMING MAP PUBLICATIONS

Call (212) 596–6139 for additional information on upcoming publications.

The Marketing Handbook is a compilation of expert advice from over twenty authorities on particular marketing strategies or tactics.

Seasonality: Managing Problems, Maximizing Opportunities is based on a survey of over 100 managing partners who shared their methods of dealing with this industry-wide problem.

Strategic Planning for CPA Firms provides a detailed approach to the design and implementation of a strategic plan that enables a firm to maximize its opportunities for growth and profits.